WITHDRAWN

HARVARD LIBRARY

WITHDRAWN

BLESSED
ELDER IAKOVOS OF EPIROS, ELDER JOSEPH THE HESYCHAST, AND MOTHER STAVRITSA THE MISSIONARY

THE OTHER VOLUMES OF THE SERIES
MODERN ORTHODOX SAINTS

Volume 1, St. Cosmas Aitolos
Volume 2, St. Macarios of Corinth
Volume 3, St. Nicodemos the Hagiorite
Volume 4, St. Nikephoros of Chios
Volume 5, St. Seraphim of Sarov
Volume 6, St. Arsenios of Paros
Volume 7, St. Nectarios of Aegina
Volume 8, St. Savvas the New
Volume 9, St. Methodia of Kimolos
Volume 10, Sts. Raphael, Nicholas, and Irene
Volume 11, Blessed Elder Philotheos Zervakos
Volume 12, Blessed Hermit Philaretos of the Holy Mountain
Volume 13, Blessed Elder Gabriel Dionysiatis

CHRIST, THE ARCHETYPE
OF SAINTS

MODERN ORTHODOX SAINTS

14

BLESSED ELDER IAKOVOS OF EPIROS, ELDER JOSEPH THE HESYCHAST, AND MOTHER STAVRITSA THE MISSIONARY

Their Life, Character, Thought, and Influence.

By

CONSTANTINE CAVARNOS

INSTITUTE FOR BYZANTINE
AND MODERN GREEK STUDIES
115 Gilbert Road
Belmont, Massachusetts 02478-2200
U.S.A.

Design and Composition:
E. Marshall Publishing & Translation Services
Brookline, Massachusetts

BX
619
.A1
C37
2000

First edition, 2000
All rights reserved
Copyright, 2000, by Constantine Cavarnos
Published by THE INSTITUTE FOR BYZANTINE AND MODERN GREEK STUDIES, INC.
115 Gilbert Road, Belmont, Massachusetts 02478-2200, U.S.A.

Printed in the United States of America

Library of Congress Control Number: 00-136581

Clothbound   ISBN 1-884729-52-5
Paperbound   ISBN 1-884729-53-3

PREFACE

In this volume, the last one of my series *Modern Orthodox Saints*, I present in concise form the life, character, thought, and influence of three recent holy personages: Elder Iakovos Valodemos of Epiros; Elder Joseph the Hesychast of the Holy Mountain of Athos; and Mother Stavritsa Zachariou, Missionary in Africa. The presentation follows a chronological sequence: Elder Iakovos was born in 1870; Elder Joseph, around 1894; and Mother Stavritsa, in 1916.

Father Iakovos stands out as a preacher and a confessor. He first became widely known to the Greek reading-public in 1955 through a series of articles that appeared in the religious monthly *Enoría* ("Parish"), under the title *Ho Patér Iákovos* ("Father Iakovos"). Eight in number, these articles were published between January 16 and June 16, 1955, six years before the Elder's death. The author of these articles was Archimandrite Haralampos Vasilopoulos. He wrote them, as he himself remarked, "in order that the rest of us might benefit by learning about his exemplary spiritual life." Following Blessed Iakovos' death in 1961, Vasilopoulos wrote and published a book devoted to him entitled *Hénas Synchronos Hágios* ("A Contemporary Saint"). In it he incorporated the entire series of articles just mentioned, added a three-page Preface, and continued his account of Father Iakovos' life from 1955 to 1961.

Archimandrite Haralampos Vasilopoulos (1910-1982) was an outstanding churchman. A biographical sketch on him appears in the Greek *Religious and Ethical Encyclopaedia* (Volume 3, 1963). He was a graduate of the School of Theology of the University of Athens, served as a preacher at many dioceses in Greece, was ordained as a priest in 1951, and in 1956 he settled in Athens, where he served as a preacher and parish priest. In 1959 he founded the "Panhellenic Orthodox Union," and in 1961 he began publishing the important monthly (later weekly) religious newspaper *Greek Orthodox Press*. In 1962 he was appointed Abbot of the Monastery Petraki in Athens. A prolific writer, besides many other works, he wrote and published 240 booklets devoted to as many saints of all periods.

In including Father Iakovos Valodemos of Epiros in the series *Modern Orthodox Saints*, I am following the discerning lead of Archimandrite Vasilopoulos, who regarded him as a saint and convincingly presented him as such in his 70-page booklet *A Contemporary Saint*. This publication is my chief source in writing about Father Iakovos. He is the second native of Epiros who is included in this series. The other is *St. Arsenios*, to whom I have devoted

Preface

Volume 6. Arsenios was born in Ioannina, the capital of Epiros.

The next figure presented in this volume, Elder Joseph the Hesychast, is widely known in Greece and America as a *hesychast*, an Orthodox Christian mystic. Having dwelt at the Holy Mountain of Athos from the age of twenty-three to the time of his death, he devoted himself particularly to the practice of mental prayer (*noerá proseuché*) and to teaching this spiritual art and the spiritual way of life in general to others—monks and laymen. I had the blessing of meeting with him in 1958, a year before his repose in the Lord, and described this meeting in my book *Anchored in God*, which was published in July 1959. This account has been incorporated in the present volume. At the end of that account I state: "During the entire conversation, Father Joseph impressed me as being a genuine mystic, a true saint." The word saint (*hósios*) was used the next year by Soterios N. Schoinas of Volos, in an article that was published in the religious bimonthly *Hagioreitiké Bibliothéke* ("Hagiorite Library"), in the September-October issue of 1959, two months after the Elder's death. For thirty years Schoinas was the editor and publisher of that journal, and personally knew Joseph very well. The Elder's two most prominent disciples, Archimandrite Ephraim, who became Abbot of the Monastery of Philotheou at Mount Athos and has established nearly a score of monasteries in

America, and Father Joseph the Younger, who is now the leading Spiritual Father of the Monastery of Vatopedi at the Holy Mountain, have each written and published a book on their Elder in which they state that they regard him as a saint.

To the above must be added the testimony of Blessed Elder Gabriel Dionysiatis, to whom I have devoted Volume 13 of the series *Modern Orthodox Saints*. In his book *Lausaïkón of the Holy Mountain*, which was published in 1953, seven years before the repose of Elder Joseph the Hesychast, Father Gabriel says:

"At the *kalyves* (monastic cottages) of Nea Skete dwells the hermit Joseph together with five of his disciples—five ascetic fathers. They had dwelt for years in caves below the Small Skete of Saint Anna. We did not have the good fortune of personally meeting with the exceedingly devout Elder Joseph. However, common opinion regards him as the most outstanding Neptic Father (*ton neptikóteron*) of our epoch, a clairvoyant (*dioratikós*), and a mystic (*hesychastés*).[1]

Missionary Mother Stavritsa, the most recent of the holy figures presented in this book, was a missionary in Africa during a period of thirty years—from 1969 to the time of her death in Kenya on

---

[1] *Lausaïkón tou Hagíou Órous*. Volos, 1953, p. 97.

Preface

January 3, 2000. Her achievements as a missionary in Kenya, Uganda, and Zaire are quite remarkable. They include, among other things, the construction or completion of nineteen churches, regular teaching of the Orthodox Faith, offering to the Orthodox there financial assistance, large quantities of icons, edifying books, food, clothing, and medicines.

Being adorned with the virtue of great humility, like the other two figures who are presented in this book, she avoided publicity. She made known what she was achieving only to organizations and persons that provided her with material resources necessary for her missionary activities. In Greece, from time to time information about her work in Africa was given to the Orthodox Missionary Brotherhood at Thessaloniki. Here in America, I called attention to her missionary activities in my book *Meetings with Kontoglou*, which was published in 1992. Following her death, highly informative and laudatory articles began to appear in religious periodicals in Greece, telling the readers about her remarkable achievements as a missionary and emphasizing her many Christian virtues: her deep Orthodox faith, her great love of God and neighbor, her benevolence, her self-sacrifice, her purity, her spirituality, and so on.

I had the blessing of meeting with Mother Stavritsa first at the Monastery of St. Raphael in Lesvos in 1964, next in Boston in 1971, and again in Boston in 1992.

In writing about her, I have drawn upon these meetings, the letters which she sent me from time to time while in Africa, and the occasional communications by telephone.

None of the figures presented in this volume has been officially recognized as a "Saint." It is perhaps too early for that. As in the case of Blessed Elder Philotheos Zervakos, Blessed Hermit Philaretos of the Holy Mountain of Athos, and Blessed Elder Gabriel Dionysiatis, also of the Holy Mountain, I present the three figures in this volume simply as "Blessed," not as "Saints." I do this for the same reason that I give in the Prefaces of the preceding three volumes of the series *Modern Orthodox Saints*.

CONSTANTINE CAVARNOS

Belmont, Massachusetts
October, 2000

CONTENTS

PREFACE vii
LIST OF ILLUSTRATIONS xv
VALUE OF READING LIVES OF SAINTS xvii

PART ONE
BLESSED ELDER IAKOVOS OF EPIROS

APOLYTIKION 19
INTRODUCTORY REMARKS 21
THE LIFE OF BLESSED IAKOVOS 25
SAYINGS OF FATHER IAKOVOS 39
APOLYTIKION TRANSLATED 41
BIBLIOGRAPHY 42

PART TWO
BLESSED ELDER JOSEPH THE HESYCHAST

APOLYTIKION 43
MY MEETING WITH BLESSED JOSEPH
    THE HESYCHAST 45
THE LIFE OF BLESSED ELDER JOSEPH 55

HIS SPIRITUAL WISDOM 73
APOLYTIKION TRANSLATED 90
BIBLIOGRAPHY 91

PART THREE
BLESSED MOTHER STAVRITSA
THE MISSIONARY

APOLYTIKION 93
MY MEETINGS WITH BLESSED
  MOTHER STAVRITSA 95
THE LIFE OF MOTHER STAVRITSA 100
HOMILY ON THE FEAST OF HOLY EPIPHANY 127
OUR SAINTS 131
BYZANTINE CHANT IN UGANDA 135
SAYINGS OF MOTHER STAVRITSA 137
APOLYTIKION TRANSLATED 141
BIBLIOGRAPHY 142
EPILOGUE 144
INDEX OF PROPER NAMES 146
INDEX OF SUBJECTS 150

LIST OF ILLUSTRATIONS

Christ, the Archetype of Saints.
    Panel icon by Photios Kontoglou.
    1954 .... Frontispiece
Blessed Elder Iakovos of Epiros.
    Photograph, *ca.* 1954 20
Father Haralampalos Vasilopoulos.
    Photograph. *ca.* 1980 22
St. Arsenios the New, a native Ioannina, Epiros.
    Icon by the monk Philateroos of the Monastery
    of Longovarda on Paros. 1961 24
Blessed Elder Joseph the Hesychast.
    Photograph, 1958 44
Nea Skete, Holy Mountain of Athos.
    Photograph 48
Father Joseph and part of his Group.
    Photograph, 1958 53
Elder Joseph when he was a young monk.
    Photograph, *ca.* 1928 59
Obituary on Father Joseph, in Greek,
    by Soterios Schoinas. Much reduced photocopy 62
Monastic Wisdom, title page of the book
    that presents Elder Joseph's Letters 67

Ékphrasis Monachikés Empeirías.
Title page of the Greek edition of *Monastic Wisdom* 68
Géron Ioséph ho Hesychastés. Title page of a book on Elder Joseph the Hesychast by his disciple Joseph the Younger 70
Blessed Mother Stavritsa, Photograph, *ca.* 1994 94
Panagia Glykophilousa, panel icon by the hand of Mother Stavritsa. 1971 99
Letter by Metropolitan Silas of New Jersey to Mother Stavritsa. Greatly reduced photocopy. 1991 126
Christ. Icon by the hand of Mother Stavritsa. 1968 130
Martyr-saints Raphael, Nicholas, and Irene. Icon by the hand of Photios Kontoglou 134

VALUE OF READING LIVES OF SAINTS

Cleave to the saints, for they who cleave to them shall be made holy.
— St. Clement of Rome

Just as painters in working from models constantly gaze at their exemplar and thus strive to transfer the expression of the original to their own artistry, so too he who is anxious to make himself perfect in all kinds of virtue must gaze upon the lives of the saints as upon statues, so to speak, that move and act, and must make their excellence his own by imitation.
— St. Basil the Great

Blessed is he who plants in his soul good plants, that is, the virtues and the lives of saints.
— St. Ephraim the Syrian

To admire the labors of saints is good; to emulate them wins salvation.
— St. John Climacos

A person is touched more profoundly and benefits more by reading one beautiful life of a saint than by discourses and philosophies.
— Agápios Landos of Athos

Eastern Orthodoxy elevates people by means of the examples of the life of the saints, and by means of holiness.
— Nicholas Berdyaev

For the Christian, there is no teaching that is more efficacious than reading the life of a saint, especially of one who has lived in his own time.
— Photios Kontoglou

PART ONE

BLESSED ELDER IAKOVOS OF EPIROS

1870-1961

Ἀπολυτίκιον

Ἦχος δ΄. Ὁ ὑψωθείς.

Ἐν ἱερεῦσιν ἱερεὺς ἀνεδείχθης,
τοῦ Βασιλέως καὶ Θεοῦ θεοφόρε,
τοὺς ἀσκητὰς μιμούμενος μακάριε·
ὅθεν συναγάλλῃ νῦν,
τοῖς χοροῖς τῶν Ἀγγέλων,
Πάτερ εὐφραινόμενος,
ἐν τοῖς ἐπουρανίοις·
Ἰάκωβε σοφὲ πνευματικέ,
σῶζε τοὺς πόθῳ,
τελοῦντας τὴν μνήμην σου.

BLESSED ELDER IAKOVOS OF EPIROS
Photograph.

Chapter 1

INTRODUCTORY REMARKS

By ARCHIMANDRITE HARALAMPOS VASILOPOULOS

On this planet where we find ourselves we are not present by chance. We have a certain purpose, a certain destiny—in fact a great destiny: *to become saints*. That is the goal of all of us. Our Creator tells us: "Become holy, for I am holy."[1]

In earlier times, very many persons struggled during their lifetime and succeeded. They became saints! They achieved holiness! Every epoch and every land can present to us many saints, known and unknown.

Our epoch appears to be sterile as far as saints are concerned. The reason for this may be the fact that people today are intoxicated by the many inventions and do not turn their attention to spiritual men.

Perhaps also people do not recognize the existing saints. Saints are not noisy. They are not like the actors, who strive to be publicized, to have their name appear in the newspapers. Saints are humble. They

---

[1] Leviticus 11:44.

FATHER HARALAMPOS VASILOPOULOS
1910-1982

avoid publicity as a temptation. Another reason perhaps why our age seems to be lacking in saints is the fact that people do not see miracles. They think that he alone is a saint who performs miracles. However, in the case of a saint a holy life is everything, miracles are not necessary.

Introductory Remarks

Nevertheless, Father Iakovos, who led a holy life in our time, and whom God deemed me worthy of seeing, of hearing, of seeking his counsel, and of dining with him, is also credited with miracles. Many miracles have been ascribed to him. This holy priest-monk dwelt during the latter part of his life at Zagorochoria of Epiros, which abounds in good and brave men. He lived at new Monodendrion at the Monastery of the Prophet Elias, which is at a mountaintop, fleeing from the deluge of sin in today's world.

All who had the good fortune of knowing him from a close distance confessed that he was a holy man. What is particularly important is that he is a *contemporary* saint.[1]

---

[1] "For the Christian there is no teaching that is more efficacious than reading the life of a saint, especially of one who has lived in his own time." —Photios Kontoglou

St. Arsenios the New

A native of Ioannina, Epiros, Arsenios became Abbot of the Monastery of St. George on the island of Paros. He died in 1877, when Iakovos of Epiros was seven years of age.

Chapter 2

THE LIFE OF BLESSED IAKOVOS OF EPIROS

By Constantine Cavarnos

*T*his very God-loving Elder was born in the village of Vodino of Argyrokastron in North Epiros, in the year of our Lord 1870. At Baptism he was given the name Evangelos. When he was tonsured a monk at the Holy Mountain of Athos his name was changed to Iakovos.

His parents (Photios was the name of his father) were pious Orthodox Christians. They were poor, and this resulted in his receiving a rather limited school education. He learned enough at school to be able to read and to appreciate religious writings.

At the age of fifteen, he went to Constantinople in order to find employment and broaden his education. In this he acted like St. Nectarios of Aegina, who at the age of fourteen left his birthplace and went to Constantinople, and during a period of eight years worked and read sacred and instructive books. Iakovos was able to earn a living by working first as a peddler and later by renting a store and selling various small articles (*psiliká*).

During this period he attended regularly and eagerly the stirring sermons of a learned priest named Konstantinos N. Kallinikos (1870-1940).[1] This priest was active in Constantinople as a catechist and preacher until the year 1904, when the Patriarchate of Constantinople assigned him as parish priest in Manchester, England. Many of Kallinikos' sermons which he heard can be found in the book *Prayer* (*Proseuché*). This was Kallinikos' first book. It was published in 1904.[2]

The sermons of Father Kallinikos had the effect of awakening Iakovos spiritually. A great event took

---

[1] Not to be confused with a younger theologian, Konstantinos Kallinikos (1912—), whose name is written without a middle initial.

[2] Among the other chief books of Kallinikos are *Sin According to the Christian View* (*He Hamartía katá ten Christianikén Antílepsin*—1919), *Christianity and War* (*Christianismós kai Pólemos*—1919), *The Christian Church and What is Performed in It* (*Ho Christianikós Naós kai ta Teloúmena en Autó*—1929), *The Psalter Interpreted in Verse* (*Ho Hierós Psaltér Emmétros Hermeneuthés*—1929). See *Threskeutiké kai Ethiké Enkyklopaideía* ("Religious and Ethical Encyclopaedia"), Vol. 7, Athens, 1965, 259-261).

The Life of Blessed Iakovos of Epiros

place within his soul: the decisive choice and resolve to live a strict Christian life. This was followed by his joining six pious young men who worked separately, having different kinds of jobs but dwelling together, and striving to grow spiritually. He did this in obedience to an experienced and wise Confessor. The young men studied religious writings together, prayed together, attended vigils together, and strictly observed the fasts ordained by the Church. They abstained from meat year-round, confessed, and received Holy Communion every week, after due preparation.

After leading this mode of life for a period of four years, he and the other members of the coenobium went to the Holy Mountain of Athos. They wanted to devote themselves to God more. With its thousands of virtuous monks, the piety and the other virtues which flourished there, the Holy Mountain was the citadel of Orthodoxy. It was there that God-loving souls sought refuge, souls that longed to attain to the heights of the virtues and of holiness. These zealous young men, having renounced worldly things, went to the Holy Mountain and became monks. Some, among them Blessed Iakovos, after their novitiate and great askesis were ordained priests.

He would have stayed there permanently, but after three years, moved by compassion for his unhappy fatherland, Northern Epiros, and wanting to benefit his fellow Christians there, he left Athos, with the blessing of his Elder, and went to Northern Epiros. There he was appointed parish priest at one of the villages near his. He dwelt at the Holy Monastery of the Theotokos which is called "Zonaria," and served as priest at that village. In this capacity, he endeavored to make known to all the will of God, which is to lead a life in accordance with the Divine Commandments.

The Turko-Albanians, being Moslems and anti-Greek, pressured the Greek population of ethnically Greek Northern Epiros. They strove to de-Hellenize and de-Christianize the Greeks. The Metropolitan of Dryinoupolis, as well as other Bishops, ordered the priests to strive to preserve the Christian and Hellenic character of the people. The priests strove successfully towards that end. Becoming aware of this, the Turko-Albanians sought to frighten them. They decided to execute two of the priests and thereby to terrify the rest in their missionary endeavor. Father Iakovos was one of those they chose to execute. They sent a detachment to capture him. Twice they came close to seizing Father Iakovos. Miraculously, he evaded their attempts.

After this, realizing that residing in Northern Epiros was no longer possible, Father Iakovos left that region and went to Zagoria, a mountainous region of

The Life of Blessed Iakovos of Epiros 29

Epiros that extents north of the city of Ioannina and includes 46 villages. In 1916, he settled near the village Monodendri, at an old deserted small Monastery named after the Prophet Elias. He worked there hard to renovate it and make it his permanent place of residence.

From time to time he brought there some young men for the purpose of preparing them for the priesthood. For he felt deeply the need of capable and virtuous priests in that region. The monastic lifestyle, he believed, which is one of privations and long prayers, was excellent training for the development of such priests.

The Metropolitan of that region conferred upon Father Iakovos the offikion of Archimandrite. However, possessing the virtue of humility, he was indifferent to this distinction. He never wore the *epanokalymmafchon*—the black veil that is put over the traditional Orthodox priest's high hat—or the large pectoral cross, customarily worn by Archimandrites.

What rendered the venerable Elder extremely valuable in that part of Epiros, where Spiritual Fathers were rare, was the practice of Confession. Many persons in the Zagorochoria and in the region of Ioannina went and confessed to him whenever he was there. Among those who confessed to him were the students of the Higher Catechetical School of the city of Ioannina. Father Iakovos urged all to confess sincerely. He told them that sins which are thus confessed are banished from the soul, whereas those not confessed remain in it, are augmented, and weigh down the soul.

Being divinely illuminated, he practiced Confession very successfully. He could discern whether those who went to him for Confession did so owing to real repentance, or out of mere curiosity or some other ulterior motive. This is why he used to say: "Many confess, but few repent." He emphasized the necessity of Repentance for fruitful Confession.

Dwelling on Confession, he used to say that the spiritual progress of a person depends on going to an experienced and wise Confessor and doing so often— at least once a month. Sincere Confession, he emphasized, frees one of the burden of sins and results in one's feeling greatly relieved. This is consonant with Christ's saying: "Come unto me, all ye that labour and are heavy laden, and I will give you rest" (Matthew 11:28).

Sometimes he served as a parish priest in various villages, when the regular priest was sick, or for some reason was absent. At such times, he handled very prudently the problems of the parishioners. And he taught them the faith, counseled them, and confessed them.

Blessed Iakovos also stressed the value of saying mentally the "Jesus Prayer." This he worded as follows: "Lord Jesus Christ, Son and Logos of God, have mercy upon me a sinner." The Jesus Prayer, he remarked, drives away from us the great tempter, Satan.

With regard to Church attendance, he recommended that people go to churches where the sermon is a regular part of the Divine Liturgy. He himself, whenever he performed this service, delivered a sermon, explaining in a simple but illuminating manner the message of the Gospel excerpt that he read, or the significance of the holy feast that was celebrated.

He spoke often about the Mysterion of Divine Communion, which is the heart of the Divine Liturgy. On such occasions he appeared transfigured, his voice expressed exultation. Divine Communion, he asserted, is an excellent means for our spiritual progress and development, and for this reason we should receive it frequently, duly prepared.

The Liturgy was not performed by him in a routine, mechanical manner, despite the fact that he officiated almost every day for sixty years. He liturgized with such attention and devoutness as if it were the first time he was doing this. He uttered the words with distinctness and duly emphasized each one of them, so that the mind could clearly follow their meaning. He succeeded, throughout the Divine Liturgy, in concentrating his mind on what he was saying and doing, not letting it wander away. Consistently with his own practice, he exhorted his congregations to be very attentive during the whole service.

His practice of always praying attentively is vividly illustrated by the following miracle. Once, during the period of civil war in Greece (1945-1949), he was walking from the village of Soudena to his Monastery, a distance of about two hours. During his walk in the wilderness he prayed mentally, as he was accustomed to do. For he had succeeded in following St. Paul's injunction: "Pray unceasingly" (1 Thessalonians 5:17). At that time the soldiers of the National Army had placed mines at a certain point of the road, and then watched from an elevated place for the passage of some rebel. Suddenly, they saw Father Iakovos approaching the spot where they had placed a mine. They screamed to prevent him from advancing there, shouting: "Father, Father." However, his attention was so focused on the prayer, that he did not hear them. He continued to walk and stepped on the mine. This exploded with tremendous force and noise, and clouds of dust rose from the spot of the explosion.

"The poor fellow is gone," said the soldiers, and they ran to the place of the mishap. When they arrived there, they could not believe what they saw. They saw the Elder all covered with dust, shaking his cassock (*rason*), without having suffered any bodily harm whatsoever.

"Haven't you suffered anything, Father?" They asked him.

"How could I, my sons?" he replied. "Can God let us suffer from anything while we are praying?"

This event took place on January 23, 1948. An account of it has been given in the periodical *Enoria*.[1]

The soul of the Elder abounded in Divine grace. With his ascetic striving—fasting, vigil, prayer—and the grace of God, he became a reborn person. He could not sin. His mind always effortlessly was turned towards God. He lived in God. He prayed unceasingly. He prayed wherever he happened to be: when he walked, when he worked, when he washed, when he dressed, when he was seated. His spirituality was above all the result of his unceasing prayer.

---

[1] January 16, 1955.

Being a man of prayer, he was a lover of church services (*akolouthías*). He recited the services at his Monastery and at the homes of the wealthy and the poor when he traveled. During his travels he had with him a bag containing the liturgical books of the Church: the *Great Horológion*, the *Parakletiké*, the *Triódion*, the *Menaía*, and so on.[1] He never missed reading the Midnight Service (*Mesonyktikón*), the Orthros, the Hours, the Vespers, and the After-the-supper Service (*Apódeipnon*).

He owed his spirituality in the next place to the Divine Mysterion of Holy Communion. At his Monastery he performed the Divine Liturgy regularly, almost every day. He began the services an hour after midnight and finished at dawn. At the Liturgy, he partook of Holy Communion.

In 1955, at the age of eighty-five, he went to the Holy Mountain to see his brother, a monk then ninety years old. He had not seen him over a period of forty years. He stayed at the Holy Mountain for two months. During his sojourn, his brother died. Father Iakovos regarded it as a blessing that he was present there and buried his brother's body with his own hands.

---

[1] About the nature of these books see my work *Byzantine Thought and Art*, pp. 109-110.

Upon his return to "the world," he received hospitality at the home of a priest named Konstantinos Bellos, at Ioannina. This priest related to Archimandrite Haralampos Vasilopoulos that he led the Elder to a room to rest during the night, and that shortly after the Elder had put out the lamp and stretched out to sleep, he went and opened the door of the room to ask the Elder if he wanted water or something else. To his great surprise, Father Bellos witnessed something miraculous. The entire face of the Elder shone, and a white light surrounded his whole body. This he took as evidence that the Elder had attained sainthood.

The same year, 1955, the Patriarch of Constantinople Athenagoras invited Father Iakovos to go there and confess the faithful during the period of the Great Lent. He went and confessed a large number of persons. Thus, his sojourn at Constantinople was a very fruitful one. This is testified to by the periodical of Patriarchate, *Apóstolos Andréas*, of April 23, 1955. It reported that the Patriarch received Archimandrite Iakovos Valodemos with great joy and reverence, offered him hospitality at the Patriarchate, and facilitated his reception of Christians for Confession at the Patriarchal Church of St. George, the Church of St. Demetrios, and other churches, as well as at the School of Theology at Halki. It says also that the Patriarch congratulated him for his service, thanked him for having gone there, and invited him to go to Constantinople again.

During his old age, Father Iakovos had often been invited to settle in the city of Ioannina, in the city of Agrinion, and in Athens, so as to live with spiritual brethren who loved him and to have all the conveniences. He declined, for he preferred the austere life of privation at his poor Monastery.

The blessed one lived for the Kingdom of Heaven, the Kingdom of God, of which he had a foretaste while here on earth. All his longing was directed to it. He meditated on it, he longed for it. He was not attached to this world in his thoughts and feelings, but steadfastly directed his aspiration to the Heavenly Kingdom.

In February of 1960 his health deteriorated. He suffered from malfunctioning of the kidneys and migraine. However, in May miraculously he became well. At the end of 1960, he became ill again and went to the hospital of Ioannina. Many went to see him and to receive his blessing. To each one he had some good words to say, words that came out of his pure and ardent heart. All believed that as on the past occasion he would miraculously become well. However, he had a presentiment of his departure from this transitory life

The Life of Blessed Iakovos of Epiros 37

to the eternal one. He died on February 15 of 1961 at the age of 91. Until then, his mind remained clear, his memory intact.

According to the instructions he had given, his body was taken and buried at his beloved Monastery of the Prophet Elias at Monodendrion in Epiros.

"His departure from this world," wrote Father Haralampos Vasilopoulos, was humble, as was his whole life. His entry into the Kingdom of God, however, was assuredly triumphal. He pleased God. And God demonstrated in this life that He accepted his struggles, for He miraculously provided His protection of him.

"Now, from the Kingdom of Heaven, where he is safe and blessed, Elder Iakovos calls out to us: "Attention, my children, beware of sin. Let not vain things lead you astray. Cultivate love of God and of neighbor. Your aim is Paradise."

The periodical *Apóstolos Andréas* wrote in its obituary among other things the following:

"Father Iakovos led an ascetic life of fasting and prayer. His conduct was irreproachable. He became the most important Confessor of his province and perhaps of all of Greece. To this unworldly Elder went with deep faith ministers, wealthy industrialists, professors, princes, and hierarchs. Peasants used to go to his humble cell even late at night and knock on the door.

"The great sanctified soul of this Priest opened the golden gate of light and repentance to a great many souls with heavy laden consciences. And he led them to a changed life.

"Some years ago he came to the Patriarchate. He reminisced his life at Constantinople when he was a young man. He experienced profound happiness when he went and prayed at the Patriarchal church and other churches. Everybody rejoiced in meeting with him and listening to his teaching.

"We learned with great sorrow that on February 15, 1961, at the age of 91, he reposed in the Lord."[1]

Father Haralampos Vasilopoulos concludes with these words his book on Blessed Elder Iakovos of Epiros, entitled *A Contemporary Saint*. "Knowledge of the life of this manifestly holy man will bring much benefit. And assuredly there will appear persons who will endeavor to imitate him to some extent in their life."[2]

---

[1] *Apostolos Andreas*, Constantinople, February, 1961.

[2] Haralampos D. Vasilopoulos, *Hénas Synchronos Hágios*, Athens, 1971, pp. 15-16.

Chapter 3

SAYINGS OF FATHER IAKOVOS[1]

The progress of a Christian depends upon his having a good Confessor (*Pneumatikós*). The Confessor must see him often, at least once a month.

***

Our time here on earth is precious. God will ask us for an account of every hour and of every minute, how we utilized it.

***

Practice the Jesus Prayer, saying: "Lord Jesus Christ, Son and Logos of God, have mercy upon me, a sinner."

***

Our heart must not be attached to anything earthly. The spiritual man looks at everything spiritually.

***

Holy Communion is an excellent means for our spiritual progress and development. With the thought

---

[1] Culled from Father Haralampos' already mentioned book, pp. 21, 23, 27, 53, 54, 62.

of receiving Holy Communion the Christian passes his time struggling spiritually and being watchful. Afterward, meditating on the fact that he has received Holy Communion and that he hosts within himself God, he is again vigilant until he begins preparation for receiving Holy Communion again. And so on.

* * *

We must not let our mind wander hither and thither during the Divine Liturgy. Instead, we must gather it together, attending to what is said and done.

* * *

Priests must exercise great attention at all times, because Satan wages war against them more than against laymen. For they are what the officers are in the army. If Satan succeeds in casting the Priests into sin, he easily ensnares the others.

APOLYTIKION

*As an emulator of the holy ascetics,
thou, O God-bearer, hast been
   worthily shown forth,
as a true priest of priests
   before the King and God.
Wherefore, thou rejoicest now
   with the choirs of the Angels,
filled with gladness and delight
   in Heaven;
O Father Iakovos, wise and spiritual,
save them who with love
   honor thy memory.*

4

BIBLIOGRAPHY

Apóstolos Andréas ("Apostle Andrew"), periodical of the Patriarchate of Constantinople, April 1955, February 1961.

Enoría ("Parish"), Athenian periodical, January 16, 1955, p. 14, February 1, p. 32, February 16, pp. 48-49, March 1, pp. 66-67, March 16, pp. 81-82, April 16, pp. 111-113, May 16, pp. 137-138, June 16, pp. 170-171.

Threskeutiké kai Ethiké Enkyklopaideía ("Religious and Ethical Encyclopaedia"), Vol. 7, Athens, 1965, 258-261.

Vasilopoulos, Haralampos, Archimandrite, *Hénas Synchronos Hágios* ("A Contemporary Saint"). Third edition, Athens, 1971, 1992.

PART TWO

BLESSED ELDER JOSEPH THE HESYCHAST
1894-1959

Ἀπολυτίκιον

Ἦχος δ΄. Ταχὺ προκατάλαβε.

Ἀσκήσει τὸ πρότερον καταδαμάσας σαρκός,
τὸ φρόνημα ὕψωσας ἐκ τῶν γηίνων τὸν νοῦν,
ὅσιε Πάτερ Ἰωσήφ.
Εἶδας τῇ θεωρίᾳ, σεσωσμένους τοὺς δήμους,
ἔδειξας τοῖς ποθοῦσι σωτηρίας τὸν τρίβον,
διὸ καὶ τοὺς τιμῶντας σε νῦν
σωθῆναι πρέσβευε.

BLESSED ELDER JOSEPH THE HESYCHAST
Photograph, 1958.

Chapter 1

MY MEETING WITH BLESSED ELDER JOSEPH THE HESYCHAST

*W*hile at Athens in 1958, I heard a great deal about two monks at Nea Skete, which lies on the southern side of the Mount Athos Peninsula, near the sea, not far from the Monastery of Saint Paul. A nephew of my publisher Alexandros Papademetriou had visited them and corresponded with them, asking for their counsel in the spiritual life. I did not miss the opportunity of going there and meeting with them during my sojourn on the Holy Mountain in May of that year.

Nea Skete is an idiorrythmic dependency of the Monastery of Saint Paul founded in the eighteenth century. At the time of my visit, it had twenty-eight *kalyves* (monastic cottages) and fifty-five monks, most of them icon painters. The rest were tailors, shoemakers, sweatermakers, and woodcarvers making small crosses, mortars, receptacles, and other beautiful artifacts.

The two monks I went to see in particular were Father Joseph the Hesychast and his disciple Hieromonk Ephraim. I met first with Elder Joseph. He was in his sixties, of short stature and medium build, with a good crop of gray hair and big, peaceful eyes. He was the spiritual father and guide of eight monks of this Skete, and was regarded by all of them with great reverence.

Father Joseph's *kalyva* was about five minutes' walk from the central church of the skete, called the *kyriakón*, and the adjacent guesthouse where I had my meals and rested during my stay at the Skete. The guestmaster notified the Elder well in advance of my planned visit to him, set the time, and guided me to the Elder's *kalyva*.

Upon seeing Father Joseph, I greeted him with the traditional, universal salutation on the Holy Mountain: "*Evlogeíte!*" ("Bless!").

To this, he responded, similarly in the traditional Athonite manner, with the words: "*Ho Kyrios.*" That is, "May the Lord bless you!"

I identified myself very briefly and stated my reason for visiting him, namely to hear what he had to say about leading a spiritual life while living in the "world," especially about the practice of mental prayer.

He led me inside his *kalyva*, a rather small house, sat on the floor, and asked me by gesture to sit down on his right side, to converse on this subject. It seems to me that he wanted our conference to take place thus seated as a lesson in humility. The virtue of humility is one which he emphasizes frequently in his Letters. The great Byzantine mystic St. Symeon the New Theologian asserts that *humility* and *faith* are the *foundation* of the spiritual life. Father Joseph shared this view.

The first thing we discussed was Confession. He began speaking as follows:

"Man cannot escape God's eye, even as regards the smallest things, even in the most secret places; for God is present everywhere. He cannot lie to God, without God knowing that he is lying. So when a person confesses, he must tell the confessor the full truth about his deeds, thoughts, and feelings, hiding nothing. Such confession is essential for one's spiritual health and progress. It is a most important means of inner purification."

Then the elder asked me if I read the *Gospels*. I replied that I did, often.

"It is good to read them daily," he said. "Read also the *Old Testament,* especially certain parts of it, such as the *Psalms*. I also strongly recommend that you read

NEA SKETE

The Elder's *kalyva* was near the tower.

My Meeting with Blessed Elder Joseph

Konstantinos Doukakis' *Great Collection of Lives of Saints* (*Mégas Synaxaristés*). It is a very comprehensive work. Recently the monk Victor Matthaiou produced a new edition of it in 14 volumes. The best time to read such writings is in the evening."

Continuing, he spoke about prayer. He said:

"Don't neglect prayer. Practice especially mental prayer, prayer of the heart, saying: 'Lord Jesus Christ, Son of God, have mercy upon me.' This is the most important form of spiritual work."

Upon hearing this, I asked him:

"But how can one practice this prayer in the world, where he is in the midst of so many cares and distractions?"

The Elder's answer was briefly this:

"Set aside an hour each day, preferably in the evening before going to bed, and practice it continuously during that time. I suggest also strongly that you read *The Way of a Pilgrim*. This book shows the importance of the prayer, and the manner in which it is to be practiced. The first part of this work is more valuable than the sequel [*i.e., The Pilgrim Continues His Way*], which seems to have been added by another author."

"Some persons say that this prayer is hazardous for one's sanity," I remarked.

"Of all forms of prayer," said Joseph, "this is the safest and best, provided it is combined with inner attention, so that the mind does not wonder off, and that one follows the instructions of an experienced spiritual guide."

"At first," he continued, "this prayer should be said *orally*. Later, it should be said *mentally*, though even then it should be said orally when one cannot concentrate too well on it. As we practice this prayer, it becomes an inner activity that goes on unceasingly. And *it gives results*. You need not accept this assertion on trust. Your own experience will prove it. Experience proves the prayer of Jesus to be very effective as a means of purifying the heart and mind, of opening up the mind and revealing to it untold spiritual treasures."

Joseph's reference to experience as a test of the value of mental prayer is quite in line, not only with the teachings of the great Byzantine mystics, but also with the modern demand for empirical verification. The recognition by the Byzantine mystics of an inner, experiential criterion is well illustrated by the following remarks of St. Nikephoros the Solitary and St. Gregory the Sinaite. "If you keep on praying in this manner," says the first, speaking about the prayer of Jesus, "the way to the heart will be opened to you....

This is beyond all doubt. We know from experience, that if you practice it with attention, the whole host of virtues will come to you: love, joy, peace, and so on."[1] His contemporary, St. Gregory the Sinaite (fl. 1330), discussing how one may avoid being led astray in matters of good and evil, stresses the value of inner experience. "Do not allow yourself," he says, "to be carried away by appearances, through light-mindedness, but remain weighty, and accept the good and reject the evil after careful testing; you ought to test and discriminate and only then believe."[2]

Continuing his talk, Father Joseph said:

"Man's *chief* aim should be to *find God*. In finding God, he finds true happiness. The interior prayer we have been discussing leads man to Him. We can never thank God sufficiently for revealing Himself to us. We can never even thank Him enough for the other goods He bestown upon us. God need not have created man: He had hosts of angels. Yet He created man and countless marvelous things for him."

I did not ask Father Joseph to tell me something about the *Typikon*, the set of rules and regulations of his Brotherhood; and he did not take the initiative in speaking on the subject. However, the subject came up

---

[1] *Philokalia*, Vol. 4, Athens, 1961, p. 28.
[2] *Ibid.*, p. 88.

in the meeting I had with his disciple Father Ephraim, whom I visited next, at the Elder's recommendation. Ephraim lived in a little hut not far from his. He was its sole occupant. With regard to the *Typikon* he gave me the following information:

All the monks under the spiritual guidance of Father Joseph—seven in number—meet with him twice a day: once at church in the morning, where they participate in the Divine Liturgy, and once at Joseph's house in the afternoon, for supper. The rest of the time they live scattered in various houses. Mental prayer occupies the most important place in their life. It is practiced by this Brotherhood around six hours continuously every morning. It takes the place of the *Orthros*. It is practiced again late in the afternoon, and takes the place of the *Apodeipnon*, the After-the-supper Service. Each monk of this group occupies himself also with a handicraft. The handicraft of Father Ephraim was carving little crosses that are hung on the neck and larger ones that are employed by priests in church services. The Elder's handicraft was making pectoral crosses and seals for stamping holy bread (*prósphora*) before it is baked.

During the entire conference I had with Father Joseph, he spoke calmly and unaffectedly. He impressed me as being a genuine mystic, a true saint.

FATHER JOSEPH AND PART OF HIS GROUP
Joseph is at the center, seated; Ephraim, in priestly
vestments, is at the extreme right.

He was not simply a contemplative. He was a practical man, too, a teacher engaged in spiritually guiding, not only his entourage, at Nea Skete, but also other monks and laymen who sought instruction and counsel through visits and correspondence. All this he did *gratis*, from his intense love of God and neighbor.

Chapter 2

THE LIFE OF BLESSED ELDER JOSEPH

*F*ather Joseph the Hesychast was born around the year 1894 in the village of Kostos in Paros, one of the Cyclades Islands in the southern Aegean Sea. Kostos was the birthplace of another outstanding holy man, Athanasios Parios (1722-1813), who in 1995 was officially recognized as a Saint by the Patriarchate of Constantinople. Athanasios Parios was a very eminent theologian and educator who flourished during the latter part of the eighteenth century and the first decade of the nineteenth.

At Holy Baptism he was named Phrangiskos. Joseph is the name he was given when he was tonsured a monk. He attended school at his native place for only two years. Then he was sent by his destitute parents to the city of Piraeus in order to work and support himself, and later to help his younger brothers and sisters. After working for years at a grocery store as an errand boy, he went to Athens and became a merchant.

Thanks to his intelligence and thrift, Phrangiskos' venture as a merchant was successful. He was able not only to send considerable financial aid home, but could also seriously hope some day to become a wealthy man.

Later, his interests began to turn away from money-making to spiritual things. One day a kindly neighbor gave him a copy of a book entitled *Kalokairiné* to read during his leisure hours. This work is comprised of the most beautiful lives of saints who are commemorated in the summer season (*kalokaíri*)—from March 1st to August 31st. The author of this book was Agapios Landos, a remarkable seventeenth century monk of Athos. Landos wrote and published other edifying books, the most famous of which is *The Salvation of Sinners*. The lives of saints narrated in *Kalokairiné* aroused Phrangiskos' interest in religion, until then dormant. He began wondering about the truthfulness of these amazing biographies.

In order to find out whether such things are possible, he started visiting popular shrines, such as the Monastery of St. Gerasimos in Kephallenia ("Cephalonia") and the Church of the Theotokos in Tinos, where miraculous events were said to occur every year. These pilgrimages had the effect of dispelling Phrangiskos' doubts or hesitations about the possibility of the miracles attributed to the saints in *Kalokairiné*. For at these holy places he both heard of similar phenomena from persons he met, and witnessed some himself.

Afterwards, he met a monk from the Holy Mountain of Athos who spoke to him about Athos and how the monks there lived. This made him eager to make a pilgrimage to Athos at his first opportunity.

His desire to go there was fulfilled at the age of twenty-three, after he had served in the Greek navy for the required period of time. Once there, he decided to stay. Having a strong aspiration to cultivate the interior life, he searched for a suitable place of quiet and a good spiritual guide. This quest led him to some of the remotest hermitages. He dwelt in succession at Katounakia, just above the awesome Karoulia, at Vigla, near the Rumanian Skete of Prodromou, again at Katounakia, at St. Basil, on the southwestern slope of Mount Carmel, at the Small Skete of St. Anna, and finally, from 1951 to the time of his repose, at Nea Skete.[1] An old hermit named Ephraim, was his best spiritual guide. Father Ephraim, a very pious and wise monk, was his Elder for years, first at Katounakia and then at St. Basil's.

---

[1] For these hermitages, see my book *Anchored in God*, where I describe my visits there.

Tonsured a monk and renamed Joseph, he led an exceedingly austere life of spiritual striving. He observed the greatest strictness in all things. Above all, he devoted himself to mental prayer, also called "spiritual prayer" and "prayer of the heart," both during the fixed periods set aside for it during the day and the night, and while he practiced his handicraft of making small wooden crosses and seals. He mastered the essentially related arts of mental prayer (*noerá euché*) and inner attention (*népsis, prosoché*) and taught them successfully to a growing number of followers. This interior life, he emphasized, constitutes the very *essence* of monasticism. It lifts the monk to the higher Christian virtues and makes him a partaker of Divine Grace.

Through this way of life, spiritual love steadily increased in him, purifying his soul and rendering it an abode of the Holy Spirit. He experienced such love for and from God that he wept copiously, overwhelmed by humility and feelings of gratitude for God's boundless love for His creatures. And he felt so much love for his fellowmen that were it possible, he would have taken upon himself the sufferings of all and died for them, in order to lift them to the blessedness of God.

His love for his fellowmen was clearly manifested not only to those who went to him and became his

ELDER JOSEPH WHEN A YOUNG MONK
Photograph. c. 1928.

disciples and lived near him, but also to numerous persons who lived in the "world"—he wrote letters to them—giving advice that evinced wisdom and deep Christian love. A great many of these letters have been gathered by some of his Athonite disciples and have been published by them.

Blessed Father Joseph became a remarkable seer and mystic. He rose to higher states of consciousness similar to those experienced by the great Orthodox mystics, the "hesychasts" of the past. By way of example, I cite the following statement from the manuscript *The Life of Our Ever Memorable Father Joseph the Hesychast*, written in 1962 by his disciple Joseph of Cyprus:

"There comes a time, as a person is practicing mental prayer with all his thoughts gathered together, invoking the sweet name of our Lord Jesus, when suddenly the mind is illumined or rather is caught by a boundless immaterial light, white as snow, and a subtle fragrance pervades all his members. And he transcends himself, stands in another creation transfigured. He no longer prays then, nor thinks, but only contemplates and marvels at the divine magnificence."[1]

---

[1] *Ho Bios tou Aeimnéstou mas Patrós Ioséph tou Hesychastoú*, Nea Skete, 1962.

Blessed Father Joseph the Hesychast reposed in the Lord on August 15 (O.S.), 1959. He had foreknowledge of this event a month before. Regarding his repose, Soterios N. Schoinas of Volos, editor and publisher of the important religious bimonthly *Hagioreitiké Bibliothéke* ("Hagiorite Library") for thirty years (1936-1965), wrote among other things the following:

"Father Joseph led a life purely Christian and ascetic. Having wholeheartedly espoused mental prayer (*noerá proseuché*), he acquired the title of 'Wakeful Father' (*Neptikós Patér*). On August 15, the feast of the Dormition of the Theotokos, he attended the Divine Liturgy and participated in the chanting. After receiving Holy Communion, he told his disciples: 'Go and take your prayer-ropes and pray that I might speedily depart; I want to hasten to our Savior Christ.'

"When they returned, shortly after that, they found him seated on his humble chair, ready to leave. After about ten minutes, he left for the Lord.

"Many days before this he had foreknowledge of his death. He called his disciples (*synodeía*) and gave them various counsels as to how to conduct themselves in order to please God.

"The death of Father Joseph is regarded as that of a saint."[1]

---

[1] *Hagioreitiké Bibliothéke*, September-October issue, 1959, pp. 343-344.

ΙΩΣΗΦ ΜΟΝΑΧΟΣ
Ἡσυχαστὴς ἐν Νέᾳ Σκήτῃ

Τὴν 15ην Αὐγούστου (π.ἡμ.) ἑορτὴν τῆς Κοιμήσεως τῆς Θεοτόκου καὶ περὶ ὥραν 9½ π. μ. ἀπῆλθε πρὸς Κύριον ὁ ἡσυχαστὴς Ἰωσὴφ Μοναχὸς Γέρων, εἰς ἡλικίαν 65 περίπου ἐτῶν.

Ὁ μεταστὰς κατήγετο ἀπὸ τὴν νῆσον Πάρον καὶ μετὰ τὴν ὑπηρεσίαν πρὸς τὴν Πατρίδα, φλεγόμενος ἀπὸ θεῖον ζῆλον πρὸς τὸ μοναχικὸν ἔνδυμα, περιεβλήθη αὐτὸ εἰς ἡλικίαν 25 περίπου ἐτῶν ἐν ἁγίῳ Ὄρει, ὑποταχθεὶς εἰς τὸν Γέροντα Ἐφραίμ, εἰς τὸ ἡσυχαστήριον Εὐαγγελισμὸς ἐν Κατουνακίοις, περιφερείας Μεγίστης Λαύρας.

Μετὰ 4 περίπου ἔτη μὲ τὸν Γέροντά του, ἀπῆλθον μαζὶ εἰς τὴν Σκήτην τοῦ ἁγίου Βασιλείου, εἰς τὸ ἡσυχαστήριον τοῦ Προδρόμου. Ἐδῶ ἀπέθανεν ὁ Γέροντάς του Ἐφραίμ. Ἐκεῖ εἰς τὸν ἅγιον Βασίλειον μὲ ὅλην τὴν συνοδείαν, συγκατελέγετο καὶ ὁ Ἀθανάσιος ὁ σαρκικὸς ἀδελφὸς τοῦ Ἰωσήφ, μὲ γέροντα πλέον τὸν Ἰωσήφ, ἥτις συνοδεία ἐξηκολούθει ἡσυχάζουσα ἐπὶ 17 ἔτη. Κατόπιν ὅλοι ὁμοῦ κατῆλθον εἰς τὴν Μικρὰν ἁγίαν Ἄνναν εἰς μέρος λίαν ἀπόκρημνον, ὅπου ἔκαμαν νέον ἡσυχαστήριον τοῦ τιμίου πάλιν Προδρόμου. Ἐδῶ ἐκάθησαν περὶ τὰ 12 ἔτη. Ἐντεῦθεν ὅλη ἡ συνοδεία ἦλθε καὶ ἐγκατεστάθη εἰς τὴν νέαν Σκήτην ὅπου ἔκαμε δύο ἡσυχαστήρια, πάλιν τὸν Πρόδρομον καὶ τὸν Εὐαγγελισμόν.

Ὁ Ἰωσὴφ ἔζησε βίον ἁγνῶς χριστιανικὸν καὶ ἀσκητικόν. Ἐνδυθεὶς ἐξ ὁλοκλήρου τὴν νοερὰν προσευχήν, ἀπέκτησε τὸν τίτλον τοῦ νηπτικοῦ πατρός. Κατὰ τὴν θείαν Λειτουργίαν τῆς Κοιμήσεως τῆς Θεοτόκου, ἣν παρηκολούθησε καὶ ἔψαλλε καὶ ἀφοῦ ἐκοινώνησε τῶν ἀχράντων Μυστηρίων, εἶπε εἰς τὰ καλογέρια του Πηγαίνετε νὰ κάμετε κομβοσχοῖνι νὰ τελειώσω γρήγορα· ἐπείγομαι νὰ μεταβῶ εἰς τὸν Σωτῆρα Χριστόν. Ὅταν μετ' ὀλίγον ἦλθον τὰ καλογέρια του, τὸν εὗρον ἕτοιμον πρὸς ἀναχώρησιν, καθήμενον εἰ τὴν πολυθρόνα του τὴν πτωχικήν. Μετὰ 10 περίπου λεπτὰ· τῆς ὥρας ἀπῆλθε πρ Κύριον.

Πρὸ πολλῶν ἀκόμη ἡμερῶν, προγνωρίσας τὸν θάνατόν του, ἐκάλεσε τὴν συνοδείαν του καὶ τοὺς ἀφῆκε διαφόρους συμβουλὰς πῶς νὰ πορεύωνται διὰ νὰ εὐαρεστήσουν τὸν Κύριον.

Ὁ θάνατος τοῦ Ἰωσὴφ θεωρεῖται θάνατος ὁσίου. Εὐχόμεθα ὁ Κύριος νὰ ἀναπαύσῃ τὴν ψυχήν του ἐν σκηναῖς ἁγίων καὶ καλὴν παρηγορίαν εἰς ἀπορφανισθέντα τέκνα του.

Σ. Σ.

OBITUARY BY SOTERIOS SCHOINAS

Hagiorite Library, September-October 1959.

(Much reduced copy.)

The Life of Blessed Elder Joseph

Soterios Schoinas knew the Elder personally very well. He visited him the day before his repose, on August 14, and asked him:

"How are you, Elder, how is your heart?"

"Tomorrow, Soterios, I am departing for the eternal fatherland. When you hear the bells ringing, recall my words."[1]

In the Preface of the same book in which these statements appear, Elder Ephraim speaks a number of times of Father Joseph as a *saint* (*hágios*), and makes the following significant remark:

"Elder Joseph was one of the greatest spiritual figures of the Holy Mountain in our time. I lived near him during a period of twelve years as his disciple. God rendered me worthy of serving him until his last breath. And he deserved every kind of service, because of his great spiritual striving and his holy prayers which he left for us as a precious heritage. We knew him as truly God-bearer (*theophóros*)."[2]

The Elder's holy way of life and character profoundly impressed and influenced many monks as well as pilgrims who visited him. Among the monks

---

[1] Archimandrite Ephraim, *Gérontos Ioséph Ékphrasis Monachikés Empeirías* ("Elder Joseph's Expression of Monastic Experience"), fourth edition, Holy Mountain, 1992, p. 23.

[2] *Ibid.*, pp. 16-17.

who particularly stand out are Elder Ephraim and Joseph the Younger of Cyprus.

Following his Elder's repose, Father Ephraim became the head of a group of eight young monks, disciples of his Elder. He considerably enlarged Father Joseph's house and vegetable garden. The handicraft of this brotherhood was making prayer ropes for monks and laymen, and small, beautifully carved wooden crosses.

As the years went by, Father Ephraim's monks increased to twenty, and his brotherhood had to move to larger living quarters. He renovated a deserted Russian Kelli at Provata, Mount Athos. Here, the brotherhood kept growing, while that of the nearby Monastery of Philotheou had seriously shrunk. It welcomed Father Ephraim and those under his direction to move into the Monastery. Moreover, he was elected its Abbot.

The population of other Hagiorite monasteries was also shrinking alarmingly, as the old monks were dying and were not being replaced by the arrival of young monks or novices. At the same time, the population of the Monastery of Philotheou, under the Abbotship of Father Ephraim, who was honored with the offikion of "Archimandrite," was fast growing. As a result, in time he succeeded in greatly increasing the number of monks at half a dozen other monasteries of the Holy Mountain by sending monks from the Monastery of Philotheou.

Then he came to America, to the United States and Canada, to confess people and establish convents and monasteries. Within a period of about twenty years, he has succeeded in establishing seventeen!

Father Joseph the Younger, the Cypriot, also acquired many followers. After the departure of Ephraim from Nea Skete, he took over the house of his Elder and enlarged it some more. He dwelt there with the young monks who were under his direction until around the year 1989. His brotherhood kept growing and had to be scattered in other monastic houses of Nea Skete. The problem of a larger dwelling place, for all of them living together, was solved when he and his brotherhood were invited to settle at the Monastery of Vatopedi—one of the oldest and largest monasteries of the Holy Mountain. He has been serving there as the leading Spiritual Father—"Starets" in Russian—of the Monastery of Vatopedi.

The beneficent influence of Blessed Joseph the Hesychast spread to other monks of the Holy Mountain, and to persons living in the "world." He deeply influenced the lives of many. At the Holy Mountain his influence has been especially through his already mentioned disciples Ephraim and Joseph the Younger. Archimandrite Ephraim has made known the teaching and example of his Elder in the "world" both through the monasteries which he has established in Greece and in America, and through the books which he published in both the Greek and the English language. In 1979, Ephraim published *Gérontos Ioséph Ékphrasis Monachikés Empeirías* ("Elder Joseph's Expression of Monastic Experience"). This work of 498 pages contains 82 Letters of his Elder. It was reprinted in 1981, 1985, and 1992. An English-language edition of it, with title *Monastic Wisdom*, was published in 1998 by St. Anthony's Greek Orthodox Monastery at Florence, Arizona, which was founded a few years ago by Father Ephraim. This work was followed the same year by a 448-page book entitled, *Counsels from the Holy Mountain*, that contains Letters and Homilies of Elder Ephraim. The teaching presented in this book is quite in line with that of Father Joseph the Hesychast, whom he mentions here and there. This work first appeared in 1989, in the Greek language, as a publication of the Holy Monastery of Philotheou, and has been reprinted several times since then.

Elder's Joseph's other outstanding disciple, Joseph the Younger, also published a volume on his Spiritual

Monastic Wisdom

The Letters of
Elder Joseph the Hesychast

ΓΕΡΟΝΤΟΣ ἸΩΣΉΦ
ἜΚΦΡΑΣΙΣ ΜΟΝΑΧΙΚΗ͂Σ ἘΜΠΕΙΡΊΑΣ

ἜΚΔΟΣΙΣ ἹΕΡΑ͂Σ ΜΟΝΗ͂Σ ΦΙΛΟΘΈΟΥ
ἍΓΙΟΝ ὌΡΟΣ ⁘ αϡοθ´ ⁘

Father, entitled: *Gerón Ioséph ho Hesychastés* ("Elder Joseph the Hesychast"), in which he gives an account of the "struggles, experiences, and teachings of his Elder. This first appeared in 1984, as a publication of the "Kellíon Evangelismós tes Theotókou" at Nea Skete. It contains a Preface by Georgios I. Mantzaridis, who was a professor at the School of Theology of the University of Thessaloniki. Professor Mantzaridis makes some remarks here which testify to the important impact of the Elder on Athonite monasticism. Thus, he says: "Elder Joseph was a simple and humble monk, who with his austere askesis and silence left very clearly the traces of his presence at the Holy Mountain. If today we have a new flowering of Hagiorite monasticism, this is due to a certain extent to Elder Joseph the hesychast.... His message is brought to us by a simple and faithful disciple of his, the monk Joseph." Before this, in 1962, Father Joseph the Younger wrote and circulated a 75-page typescript entitled *The Life of Our Ever-memorable Father Joseph the Hesychast*, to which I made reference earlier.

These books of Fathers Ephraim and Joseph the Younger are read at the Holy Mountain and in the "world." They undoubtedly exercise a very beneficial influence on both monastics and laymen.

ΙΩΣΗΦ ΜΟΝΑΧΟΥ

ΓΕΡΩΝ ΙΩΣΗΦ Ο ΗΣΥΧΑΣΤΗΣ

ΑΓΩΝΕΣ - ΕΜΠΕΙΡΙΕΣ - ΔΙΔΑΣΚΑΛΙΕΣ

(+1959)

ΑΓΙΟΝ ΟΡΟΣ 1984

Among those living in the "world" who were profoundly influenced by Elder Joseph's letters was his niece Vryenni. She sought through correspondence his counsels on the spiritual life, and he responded again and again to her letters. After a time she espoused the monastic life, and in time became the Abbess of a convent in Attica. Many years ago, I visited the convent and talked with Mother Vryenni about her holy uncle Joseph. She told me that she had many letters of spiritual counsel that he had sent to her, and she treasured them. Some of these letters have been translated into English and been included in the already mentioned book *Monastic Wisdom*, which has the subtitle, "The Letters of Elder Joseph the Hesychast."

Another noteworthy person who was deeply influenced by the example and teaching of Elder Joseph the Hesychast was Dionysios Batistatos, a brother of Vryenni. Batistatos became a prominent theologian and religious writer of traditionalist orientation.

Among his valuable contributions to Greek Orthodox literature is a two-volume edition of Palladios' *Lausiac History* prepared by him and the theologian N. Th. Bougatsos. This presents the ancient Greek text, a translation of it into modern Greek *katharevousa*, together with an Introduction and comments. It contains the lives and teachings of numerous early Desert Fathers and Mothers. Father Joseph was fond of reading the Lives of Saints and the Sayings of the Desert Fathers; and he himself was a Desert Father. It is not by mere chance that his nephew Dionysios Batistatos undertook the production of this very edifying work.

Here in America, the influence of Elder Joseph the Hesychast is discernible not only in the life and activities of his disciple Archimandrite Ephraim, but also in those of Archimandrite Panteleimon, founder of Holy Transfiguration Monastery in Brookline (a suburb of Boston), Massachusetts. A photograph of the Elder is prominent at that Monastery. Father Panteleimon visited him briefly in 1957, and in 1958 received from him instruction and exhortation during a three-week sojourn at Nea Skete. He found the Blessed Elder's character, teaching, and way of life illuminating and inspiring, and had the desire to join the community at Nea Skete but was prevented by various circumstances.

Chapter 3

HIS SPIRITUAL WISDOM

Since the appearance of my book *Anchored in God* (1959), where I devote a chapter to my 1958 meeting with Blessed Elder Joseph the Hesychast and his disciple Hieromonk Ephraim, readers of that book have been asking me from time to time for additional information about Father Joseph. Some want to learn more about my meeting with him; others, to know if any of his writings have been published in English translation.

Such questions increased after the publication of my second book on Athos, entitled *The Holy Mountain*, in 1973. In it I devote several pages to Father Joseph, presenting his biography, deriving my data from the already referred to typescript, *The Life of Our Evermemorable Father Joseph the Hesychast.*[1]

The recently published book, *Monastic Wisdom*, constitutes the best response to the questions raised by

---

[1] *The Holy Mountain*, pp. 69-72.

the readers of my above-mentioned books. And I am sure it will be received with great joy by all persons who are sincerely interested in authentic Orthodox spirituality. It is comprised of Eighty-two Letters, most of them addressed to monks and nuns who sought the Elder's spiritual guidance. Taken together, they constitute a great treasury of teachings on the spiritual life. They provide valuable instruction on many phases of it. This instruction is based on the Holy Scriptures, the writings of the Holy Fathers of the Orthodox Church, the lives of saints, and on the Elder's own life as a spiritual striver and guide at the Holy Mountain.

In order to properly understand his teaching, it is best to begin by taking note of the written sources of his teaching and some of his exemplars among the saints of the past. As far as writings are concerned, Father Joseph mentions here and there the following:

(1) *Holy Scripture,*

(2) *The Ascetical Homilies of Saint Isaac the Syrian,*

(3) *The Spiritual Homilies of Saint Macarios the Egyptian,*

(4) *The Contrite Discourses of Abba Dorotheos,*

(5) *The Evergetinos,*

(6) *The Philokalia,*

(7) *The Sayings of the Desert Fathers,*

(8) Books of *Lives of Saints*,
(9) *The Way of a Pilgrim*, and
(10) *The Salutations to the Theotokos*.

About the *Holy Scriptures*, he says: "Always have the *New Testament* in your pocket, and when you find a brief opportunity read an excerpt. Thus Christ gives you light and guides you towards His commandments. He completes your love and guides you to imitate Him" (Letter 78). About the *Old Testament*, he says: "Piously read the *Old Testament* and you will extract the divine nectar of faith and love. In it God spoke directly to men, and angels guided them" (*ibid.*). In the letters there are innumerable quotations from the *Holy Bible*.

About *The Ascetical Homilies of Saint Isaac the Syrian* and *The Spiritual Homilies of Saint Macarios the Egyptian*, Father Joseph remarks: "Purchase these books and you will greatly benefit" (Letter 2). Recommending Abba Dorotheos' book, he says that it "is very contrition-evoking, well written, and of great spiritual benefit" (Letter 16).

Speaking of the *Evergetinos*, he says: "There you will find many stories that will benefit you greatly" (*ibid.*). This monumental Byzantine work of the eleventh century presents teachings and instructive incidents of hundreds of early Desert Fathers and some Desert Mothers.[1]

From *The Sayings of the Desert Fathers* the Elder quotes among other sayings this striking statement: "An angry and irritable man is not accepted in the Kingdom of God, even if he raises the dead!" (Letter 6).

He recommends again and again reading the lives of Saints. In one of his Letters he remarks: "The lives of Saints and the writings they left us warm up the fervor of your soul, incite it to desire ardently our sweetest Jesus, just as officers in the army tell their troops about the feats of the brave and thus make them fight valiantly" (Letter 11). In another Letter he says: "Read the lives of Saints and see how many hardships they endured against their 'old-man'" spoken of by Saint Paul in Romans 6:6 (Letter 23). And in still another Letter he says: "If you read the lives of saints and toil (pray) a little at night, you will quickly obtain what you seek, and your soul will rejoice that Christ loves you so much" (Letter 77).

About the book *The Way of a Pilgrim*, the Blessed Elder advises one of his spiritual children to acquire copies of it and distribute them to Christians, that they

---

[1] I discuss it in Vol. 1 of my *New Library*, pp. 46-49.

His Spiritual Wisdom 77

might benefit spiritually (Letter 78). It is worth noting that in my meeting with him, which I describe in *Anchored in God,* Father Joseph said to me: "I suggest strongly that you read *The Way of a Pilgrim.* This book shows the importance of mental prayer, or prayer of the heart, and the manner in which it is to be practiced. The first part of this work is more valuable than the sequel, which seems to have been added by another author."

With regard to *The Salutations to the Theotokos,* he advises: "Read them, and she will always guard you from every evil" (Letter 78).

All reading of edifying writings, he emphasizes, "should be done *with much attention,* so that with all this the soul may increase and grow. Thus the 'old man' will fade away and die, whereas the 'new man' will grow and overflow with the love of Christ. Then a person is no longer pleased at all with earthly things, but continuously hungers for the heavenly" (Letter 5).

Also important for properly understanding the Elder—besides the writings he recommended for reading—is taking note of some of the saints he particularly admired. He mentions Isaac the Syrian, Andrew the "fool for Christ," Antony the Great, Arsenios the Great, Lukas of Steiron, Macarios the

Egyptian, Mary the Egyptian, Nectarios of Aegina, Onouphrios, and Peter the Athonite.

He calls Abba Isaac the Syrian "the boast of hesychasm and the consolation of ascetics, who assures and encourages spiritual strivers more than all the other Fathers do" (Letter 82, Chapter VI).

St. Nectarios is characterized by the Elder as a great Saint. He notes that he read Nectarios' Letters and learned from him, among other things, the need of paying attention to doctors and medicines. "During my earlier period," remarks Father Joseph, "I wanted to heal only through faith. But now I, too, am learning that both medicines and grace are necessary." From Saint Nectarios he also learned the importance of watching one's diet. Thus, he tells one of his spiritual children: "Take control of your appetite: don't eat things that you know are harmful to your health: fried foods, sauces, pork, meats, salted fish, and alcoholic beverages in general" (Letter 49).

About Saints Antony the Great, Onouphrios, Mary the Egyptian, and Luke of Steirion, he remarks that they were highly gifted mentally and "were taught by God, receiving teachings from God without a teacher" (Letter 3). However, he emphasizes that generally a spiritual striver needs a wise and experienced guide, in

His Spiritual Wisdom

order to tread safely and successfully the path that leads to purity and spiritual perfection.

The *beginning* of the path is *self-examination* with a view of *self-knowledge*. "Know thyself" is a phrase that appears in several of the Letters. "The first and foremost step" that one must take, says Father Joseph, "is to 'know oneself.' That is, to know who you really are in truth, and not what you imagine you are. With this knowledge you become the wisest man. With this awareness, you reach humility and receive grace from the Lord. However, if you don't obtain self-knowledge, but consider only your toil, know that you will always remain far from the path" (Letter 3). Knowing yourself consists in knowing "your weaknesses, passions, and shortcomings" (*ibid.*).

The Elder places great emphasis on the need of becoming *aware* of your "passions" and proceeding *to struggle to overcome them*, to *free* yourself from them, to attain *passionlessness*, which means *purity*. This high spiritual state can only be attained, he stresses, by *persistent struggle* and *Divine grace*.

"Passion" (*pathos*) in Orthodox Patristic writings is a term used in two senses: (a) to denote *bad thoughts* (*logismoí*) *charged with emotion*, and (b) *vices* (*kakíai*), that is, such thoughts become *habits*, settled dispositions of the soul, bad traits of character.

The passions particularly discussed by the Blessed Father are the following: (1) *pride*, (2) *despondency*, (3) *sorrow*, (4) *lust*, (5) *anger*, and (6) *sloth*.

In one of his Letters he calls attention to the fact that *pride* engenders *hardness*, *disobedience* and *scandals*, and results in a man's *fall*. He quotes the saying of the Holy Fathers that "Pride goeth before a fall, and humility before Grace" (Letter 32).

He speaks often of *despondency* or *despair*, and characterizes it was a "mortal sin." "The Devil," he remarks, "rejoices in it more than in anything else" (Letter 18). Despondency is a result of pride; it is not found in a person who is humble. As soon as a proud person falls into sin, he also falls into despair, hardens, makes no effort to rise; whereas a person who possesses humility will rise again and again. So Father Joseph advises: "Don't despair because you sinned,... but exert yourself to obtain humility, and confess your sin. Despair is banished immediately through Confession" (Letter 18).

Speaking about another passion, *sorrow*, the Elder remarks that sorrow fills the soul with bitterness and gives birth to many evils (Letter 19). "Excessive sorrow can sometimes cause insanity," he notes (Letter 65). Therefore, he counsels: "Don't be sad. Don't despair. Take courage. Cast away the grief from your

His Spiritual Wisdom 81

soul." And as in the case of despondency, he advises Confession. "When a person confesses, his soul is cleansed and become like a brilliant diamond" (Letter 66).

Father Joseph makes reference to "the passion of the flesh called *lust*." He relates it particularly to demonic influence, and mentions hardships and prayer as the therapy (Letter 18; cf. Letter 55).

About the passion of *anger*, we have already noted the statement which he quotes from the Desert Fathers: "An angry and irritable man is not accepted in the Kingdom of Heaven, even if he raises the dead." And he advises everyone: "Never seek to correct each other with anger, but with humility and sincere love. Since man was created rational and gentle, he is corrected far better with love and gentleness than with anger and harshness" (Letter 6). "When you see anger ahead, forget about correcting a person at that moment" (*ibid.*).

He makes reference to *sloth* (Letter 55), and emphasizes the need of its opposite: *zeal* or *fervor*. We have noted that one of the benefits derived from *reading the lives of Saints*, mentioned by him, is that it "warms up the fervor of the soul."

All the "passions" are viewed by Father Joseph as *diseases* of the soul in need of *therapy*. Removing them from the soul is a process he calls—as do the Holy Fathers of the past—*purification*. This restores the soul to a state of health and peace. "The more you are purified from the passions, the more peace you have, the wiser you are, the more you understand God" (Letter 65).

Therapy of the passions is effected by the following means that are mentioned and discussed in the Letters:

(1) *Fasting*, (2) *vigil*, (3) *prayer*, especially mental prayer or prayer of the heart ("Lord Jesus Christ, Son of God, have mercy upon me"), (4) *inner attention* or *watchfulness*, (5) *guarding of the five senses*, (6) *meditation*, "bringing to mind various beneficial thoughts: death, hell, the Judgment at the Second Coming of Christ, Paradise, the enjoyments of the righteous, the eternal blessings" (Letter 82, Chapter I), (7) *Repentance*, (8) *Confession*, (9) *frequent Holy Communion*, (10) *zeal* or *spiritual fervor*,

Success is attained by these when the striver is helped by Divine grace, called by the Elder "purifying grace." This "mystically helps the struggling penitent to be purified of sins and to be in the state *according to nature*.... For the passions entered the nature of man after Adam's disobedience, whereas the *natural state* in

His Spiritual Wisdom 83

which man was created by God was passionless" (Letter 82, Chapter XI).

Blessed Father Joseph distinguishes *three stages of the spiritual Life*: (1) the stage of *purification*, which has already been discussed, (2) the stage of *illumination*, and (3) the stage of *perfection*. The second and the third stages lift man to a state *above nature*.

During the stage of *illumination*, the mind is illuminated by "*illuminating grace* and *perceives everything clearly*. One receives *the light of knowledge* and is raised to *the vision of God*. This does not mean seeing illusory lights, fantasies, and images; it means radiance of the mind, clearness of thoughts, and depth of ideas.... The mind receives Divine illumination and becomes entirely Divine light, by which one mentally perceives the truth and discerns how he must proceed until he reaches Love, which is our sweet Jesus" (Letters 2 and 12.XI).

"The third stage of the spiritual life is that of the *grace of perfection*" (Letter 2). This grace perfects the spiritual striver. It wipes out all the passions and preserves all the virtues as parts of one's nature, without one needing to use his own devices and methods to do this (Letter 82.XI). The virtues, adds the

Elder, render the possessor of them "in the likeness of God" (Epilogue).

With regard to the last point, it should be explained that following the great Holy Fathers of Orthodoxy, he distinguishes between being "in the likeness of God" from being "in the image of God." The latter expression denotes the possession of a rational soul; "in the likeness of God" refers to the possession of the totality of the virtues in highly developed permanent form.

At the stage of perfection, of "perfecting grace," there is a blossoming of the virtues of wisdom, discernment, humility, patience, chastity, courage, gentleness, obedience, temperance, spiritual love, and the other virtues. Father Joseph mentions most often the virtues just named.

Wisdom, as this term is used here, includes faith, spiritual knowledge and illumination, and excludes ignorance, false belief, heresy or error. The Blessed Elder says characteristically: "Flee from ignorance, the mother of all evil. Ignorance of what is good is darkness of soul" (Letter 18). As we noted earlier, he regards *self-knowledge* as a very important form of wisdom. "Discernment" is another very important form of wisdom. Thus, he says: "Discernment sees, measures, and weighs" (Letter 82,V). "Knowledge" destroys and abolishes every evil and proud thought (Letter 82.IV).

Patience is a virtue that is also duly emphasized. Father Joseph says: "One's spiritual state and the grace he has are testified to by his patience" (Letter 7). He quotes Christ's statement: "In your patience possess ye your souls" (Luke 21: 19). And he adds: "Without patience it is impossible for a person to triumph. A monk without patience is a lamp without oil" (Letter 37).

He extols *chastity*. Thus, in one of his letters he says: "I do not know of anything else that pleases our sweet Jesus and His All-blameless Mother more than chastity and virginity. Whoever desires to enjoy their great love should see to it that he makes his soul and body pure and chaste. Thus will he receive every heavenly good" (Letter 35).

Courage is a virtue that is often mentioned in his Letters. He says: "Acquire a brave spirit against the temptations that come.... Forget what your despondency and indolence tell you. Don't be afraid of them. Just as the previous temptations passed away with the grace of God, these, too, will pass" (Letter 20). Again he exhorts: "Give courage to yourself, for joy and comfort will come to you. 'Be brave, my soul,' you should say, this is only a temptation, a trial, an affliction. Afterwards you will have peace and joy and grace for many days" (Letter 23).

He counsels his spiritual children to cultivate the virtue of *gentleness*. Thus, he says: "With whatever gentleness you use in speaking to others, that very same gentleness will Christ use with you.... Just as you forgive the failings of others, He forgives yours" (Letter 71).

Obedience is often mentioned as a very important virtue: obedience to God's commandments and to one's Spiritual Father. Through obedience, he points out, "we purify ourselves from various passions, from arrogance and complacency with our own will, so that we may receive Divine grace" (Letter 82.VII).

Temperance, the avoidance of extremes, is a virtue that the Elder emphasizes in his later Letters. In his early period as a spiritual striver, he tended towards extremes in his fasting, vigils, and other hardships. This caused permanent damage to his bodily health, and led him later to advise his spiritual children to observe *moderation*. We see this in his 54th and 55th Letters, and most emphatically in the 82nd. In the latter, he says: "A monk must guard himself from extremes and walk in the middle way: he must incline neither to the right nor to the left" (Chapter X). He

His Spiritual Wisdom 87

notes that only when one has made great progress in the spiritual life can the body bear extreme hardships.

The virtue of *spiritual love*, which for the Christian is the highest of the virtues, is discussed at some length in the last chapter of the last Letter, the 82nd. Interestingly, this parallels the treatment of it by St. John Climacos in his *Ladder of Divine Ascent*. St. John discusses it at length in the last Discourse or Step of the *Ladder*, the 30th. The reason for this is the fact that although spiritual love is the *highest* of the virtues in the *order of value*, in its *fully developed* state it is the *last in the order of acquisition*. This is the love enjoined by Christ in His two Commandments: "Thou shalt love the Lord thy God with all thy heart, and with all thy soul, and with all thy mind, and thou shalt love thy neighbor as thyself." The Blessed Elder says that all men are able to fulfill these commandments if they choose and firmly resolve to do so.

This is not the only kind of spiritual love. There is another, which is still higher, says Father Joseph: Divine love. This love does not depend on our will, but comes from God to man. "It depends on the fountain of Love, our sweetest Jesus, Who gives us if He wants, how He wants, and whenever He wants" (Letter 82.XII). When His Love descends upon a person, he can hardly endure its Divine action, and cries out:

"What shall separate me from Thy sweet Love, O Jesus?" (*ibid.*).... As he says this, the wind of the Spirit blows upon him with His marvelous and ineffable fragrance; the senses cease, not permitting any bodily action at all. And entirely captivated and closed up in silence, he can only marvel at the riches of the glory of God" (*ibid.*).

The orientation of the Letters assembled in the book *Monastic Wisdom* is manifestly what is called "otherworldly." The goals set by Blessed Father Joseph the Hesychast are all spiritual. They are set by one who sees human life *under the aspect of eternity*. Man's most precious possession is his *soul*, which is *immortal*; he *must take care of it.* The Elder writes in one of his Letters: "I earnestly entreat you: take care of your souls" (Letter 29). And he explains throughout his 82 Letters *what* he means by "taking care of the soul." It means preeminently striving to *purify* it of all the *passions* and *vices*, and to *adorn* it with all the *virtues*, which *perfect* it as far as is possible during our life on the earth.

He who cares for his soul in such a manner will abide in peace and contentment in this world and may justly expect to fare well in the life beyond death. Thus, Father Joseph says: "When the hour of death comes, as soon as these eyes close, the inner eyes of the soul will open. And as it contemplates the things 'there,' suddenly it finds itself in those things it longs for, without realizing how. It passes from darkness to light" (Letter 38). "As from sleep, we shall wake up into the other life. Then we will see parents, brothers, relatives. Then we will see angels and saints.... We shall converse with them as with brothers, giving one another a divine embrace, and continuously wondering at the heavenly choirs, until we reach our Master and Savior, and thenceforth remain inseparable" (Letters 40, 47).

APOLYTIKION

Having subdued the flesh
by thine ascetical life,
thou didst lift thy mind and thought
from the things of the earth,
O Joseph, our righteous Father.
Thou didst see in divine vision
the assembly of the saved;
thou didst show the path of salvation,
to them that desired it.
Wherefore, do thou now intercede
for those who honour thy memory.

BIBLIOGRAPHY

Cavarnos, Constantine, *Anchored in God*: Life, Art, and Thought on the Holy Mountain of Athos. First edition Athens, 1959. Reprinted in Belmont, Massachusetts 1975, 1991, 1995.

Cavarnos, Constantine, *The Holy Mountain of Athos*. First edition Belmont, Massachusetts, 1973. Reprinted 1977, 1988. Greek-language edition, Athens, *To Hágion Óros*, 2000.

Ephraim, Archimandrite, *Patrikaí Nouthesíai* ("Fatherly Counsels"). Holy Mountain, Monastery of Philotheou, 1989. English-language edition, *Counsels from the Holy Mountain*, Florence, Arizona, St. Anthony's Greek Orthodox Monastery, 1999.

Gabriel Dionysiatis, Archimandrite, *Lausaïkón tou Hagíou Órous* ("Lausaïkon of the Holy Mountain"). Volos, 1953.

Hagioreitiké Bibliothéke ("Hagiorite Library"), September-October, 1959, pp. 343-344.

Joseph, Monk, the Younger, *Ho Bíos tou Aeimnéstou mas Patrós Ioséph tou Hesychastoú* ("The Life of Our Evermemorable Father Joseph the Hesychast"). Holy Mountain, Nea Skete, 1962.

Joseph, Monk, the Younger, *Géron Ioséph ho Hesychastés* ("Elder Joseph the Hesychast"). Holy Mountain, Nea Skete, Kellion Evangelismos tes Theotokou, 1981.

Joseph the Elder, the Hesychast, *Ekphrasis Monachikés Empheirías* ("Expression of Monastic Experience"). Preface and Introductory Remarks by Archimandrite Ephraim. Holy Mountain, Publication of the Holy Monastery of Philotheou, 1979. Reprinted 1981, 1985, 1992. English-language edition, *Monastic Wisdom*: Letters. Preface by Archimandrite Ephraim and Prolegomena by Constantine Cavarnos. Florence, Arizona, St. Anthony's Greek Orthodox Monastery. 1998.

PART THREE

BLESSED MOTHER STAVRISTA THE MISSIONARY
1916-2000

Ἀπολυτίκιον

Ἦχος πλ. δ΄.

Ἐν σοὶ Μῆτερ ἀκριβῶς,
διεσώθη τὸ κατ' εἰκόνα·
λαβοῦσα γὰρ τὸν σταυρόν,
ἠκολούθησας τῷ Χριστῷ,
καὶ πράττουσα ἐδίδασκες,
ὑπερορᾶν μὲν σαρκός,
παρέρχεται γάρ·
ἐπιμελεῖσθαι δὲ ψυχῆς,
πράγματος ἀθανάτου·
διὸ καὶ μετ' Ἀγγέλων συναγάλλεται,
ὁσία Σταυρίτσα τὸ πνεῦμα σου.

BLESSED MOTHER STAVRITSA
With Bishop Theodoros Nankyama of Uganda
and the Greek Consul of Uganda. *Ca.* 1994.

Chapter 1

MY MEETINGS WITH BLESSED MOTHER STAVRISTA

I first met with Mother Stavritsa Zachariou in the fall of 1964 at the Monastery of St. Raphael, which is near the village of Thermi on the island of Lesvos. The previous year she had brought a number of holy icons done by her hand as gifts to the Monastery. I learned from her about her life and spiritual aspirations. She lived and worked at that time in the City of New York. I invited her to visit me and my mother and sister at our home in Belmont, Massachusetts.

She visited us in the summer of 1971. To my great surprise, she brought as a gift a beautiful icon done by her hand depicting the Theotokos and the Child Christ.

About this icon, which is of the type called *Panagia the Glykophilousa* ("The Sweetly Loving All-Holy Mother"), Stavritsa made the following very touching statements in a letter which she wrote after her return to New York:

"I am very glad that you like and venerate the icon which I presented to you. You may be certain that whatever you say to the Theotokos before this icon she will listen to, because it was her will to come near you. Also, you may be sure that she will help you and protect you from every evil."

This icon is a masterpiece. It is similar to an icon of the Theotokos which was done by Photios Kontoglou in 1955 and has been since that year at my home. Kontoglou's Panagia the Glykophilousa arrived at my home likewise as a great surprise—without my having ordered it or expected it. He had done it for the Greek church at Denver, Colorado, and had shipped it there together with other icons which he had done for the iconostasis. But those who had ordered the icons did not like them; they wanted icons of the modernistic, naturalistic style. So Kontoglou asked them to ship the icons to me; and he entrusted me to take them to Archbishop Michael in New York. He was to ship them to Athens by one of the Greek oceanliners, which at that time made regular trips from New York to Piraeus. Kontoglou suggested that I might keep two or more of the icons which I particularly liked and asked me to keep one of them as a gift. I selected the icon of the Panagia the Glykophilousa and the icon of the Transfiguration of Christ. Both are superb works.

My Meetings with Blessed Mother Stavritsa 97

My third meeting with Blessed Mother Stavritsa took place in 1991. She came to my home and stayed for three days as a guest of my sister, my brother, and myself. (Our mother had reposed in the Lord in 1981.) We listened to her, deeply moved, describe in detail her activities and achievements as a missionary in Africa, the problems she encountered, and the various needs.

In response to some of the needs to which she called attention, I promised to ship to her many of my publications for free distribution, and I suggested that we visit Holy Transfiguration Monastery, which is only a few miles from my home, for a supply of icons, incense, and candles. She knew and esteemed the founder of the Monastery, Archimandrite Panteleimon, and at once assented to my suggestion. We went to the Monastery and were warmly received. The Elder was aware of Mother Stavritsa's missionary activities, her love of Byzantine iconography and use of it, and her need of incense and candles. He instructed the monks to fill two large cartons with beautiful traditional paper icons printed in color, and with fragrant incense (*moschothymíama*), and another carton with beeswax candles. All these gifts were the handiwork of the monastic community. They were carefully packed at the Monastery, ready to be shipped by parcel post to Missionary Stavritsa's address at Nairobi, Kenya.

When they arrived there, many months later, they occasioned great joy. Thus, she wrote to me:

"I have received the three cartons, containing the incense, the icons, and the candles. I thank you very much for everything. Please convey to the very reverend Father Panteleimon the thanks of all of us. Our Christians here rejoice when I give them such beautiful icons; the priests experience great joy for the beautiful incense. I distributed the candles on the feast of the Holy Theophany. Everyone held a lit candle during the ceremony of the Great Blessing of the Water in the Church of St. Luke the Apostle."

One of the days of Mother Stavritsa's sojourn with us happened to be Sunday, and we went together with her to the Church of Sts. Constantine and Helen in Cambridge, Massachusetts, where the parish priest, Rev. Dr. Asterios Gerosterios, had invited her to be a special guest. At the end of the Divine Liturgy Father Asterios asked her to speak to the congregation about her activities as a missionary in Africa. She spoke in an illuminating and moving manner that enthused all present. At the end, many approached her and congratulated her for the important God-pleasing work which she was doing and encouraged her to

My Meetings with Blessed Mother Stavritsa

PANAGIA GLYKOPHILOUSA
By the hand of Mother Stavritsa, 1971.

continue it. Also, spontaneously a substantial collection was made as a very tangible form of encouragement.

Chapter 2

THE LIFE OF MOTHER STAVRITSA

*F*ervent Missionary Mother Stavritsa Zachariou was born in 1916 in the city of Kydoníai—also known as Aïvalí—which is on the west coast of Asia Minor, across from the historical island of Lesvos. Her parents were well-to-do. Her father, Demetrios Kyrlís, was killed by the Turks in 1922, during the Asia Minor catastrophe. At that time, a million and a half of Greeks who lived in Asia Minor were either slaughtered by the Turkish armies, or were permanently expelled from their ancestral homes and shrines, and found refuge in the Greek islands and mainland.

With her mother and sister, she escaped to Mytilene, the capital of Lesvos. After a period of time, they went to Komotiní, a city north of Mytilene, in the Greek mainland named Thrace. She attended there the gymnasion (high school) for two or three years. This education was of a high order, judging from her letters to me, which are written orthographically and in a clear, organized manner.

At the age of sixteen, Stavritsa returned to Mytilene and settled there. She received instruction in the art of designing clothes and sewing, mastered these arts, and by practicing them she had a very good income.

After about twenty-five years in Mytilene, she moved to Athens. There she lived for about a year in a house next door to that of Photios Kontoglou, the famous iconographer and writer. Kontoglou and his wife, Maria, were natives of Kydoníai; and this served as a special bond of friendship between Stavritsa and them. She used to go with him and his wife to the Church of St. Catherine in that vicinity on feast days according to the Old Calendar, which that parish followed, as well as at other times. Sometimes on Sundays they went to the Church of Saint Barbara at Ano Patésia, and occasionally to the Byzantine Church of Kapnikaréa at Athens. Kontoglou always took part in the chanting, according to her testimony.

At times she watched Kontoglou paint icons at his home, doing them in the Byzantine style, which with his unrelenting struggles he had succeeded in reviving. She did not have then an incentive to try to learn Byzantine iconography, and hence received no instruction in it from this master. However, his art, life and thought were destined to exercise an important influence on her throughout her life. In the talks I had with her, and in her letters, she often mentioned Kontoglou with expressions of the highest esteem.

Mother Stavritsa married a Greek-American, surnamed Zachariou, and came with him to the United States around 1950. They settled in New York City. Soon she found employment with New York furriers—designing, making, and selling fur garments. Her income was very good.

After about ten years her husband died. Then, her only child, her son, married and settled in Florida. She was left alone, but not without high aspirations. She began thinking seriously of espousing either the monastic life or that of a missionary, for she had a strong inclination for both.

During this period of loneliness and indecisiveness, she learned about Kontoglou's remarkable book *Semeíon Mega*, "A Great Sign," which was first published in early 1962 at Athens.

In this book, Kontoglou's most popular one, are described in detail a great number of supernatural events that took place at Thermí, a village on the eastern side of Lesvos, across from Kydoníai. These events are related above all to St. Raphael, who was

Abbot of a monastery near that village, at a site called Karyes. St. Raphael suffered martyrdom there by the Turks in 1463, ten years the fall of Constantinople.

According to accounts given in *Semeíon Méga*, beginning with the year 1959, St. Raphael and others who suffered martyrdom there appeared in visions and dreams to many residents of Thermi and elsewhere. Kontoglou's book prepared the way for the establishment of a convent at the site of the martyrdom and of the monastery that had been headed by St. Raphael and was destroyed by the Turks in 1463. The new monastery was named after St. Raphael.

On September 12, 1962, the Greek Ministry of Education, following the proposal of the Holy Synod of the Church of Greece, issued a decree by virtue of which there was founded a monastery for women near the village of Thermí, at the site of the destroyed monastery. Soon the foundation of the church of the convent began to be laid, and cells to be built for the nuns who were expected to go and settle there.

Mother Stavritsa learned about Kontoglou's book *A Great Sign*. Many thousands of copies were sold in Greece and abroad. She bought a copy and read it deeply moved. This prompted her to make a generous contribution towards the building of the convent. In the book *Karyes, the Hill of the Saints*, written by Vasilikí Rálli, we read:

"Many of the Greeks in America contributed to the dear-to-God undertaking of the construction of the convent—one of them was Stavritsa Zachariou, a resident of New York, now a missionary in Africa."[1]

Stavritsa went to Karyes around 1962 to venerate the sacred relics of the martyrs Raphael, Nicholas and Irene, and to sponsor the Baptism of orphans. She became the godmother of forty babies!

Greatly enriched spiritually she returned to New York. Although she continued to work as a furrier and had no financial problems, her mind was more and more directed to spiritual things. She increasingly detached herself from worldly-minded persons, prayed more, and attended Church services with greater regularity. All these things brought her closer to the martyr-saints of Thermi, Lesvos. Thus, according to her account, while in her apartment, St. Raphael appeared to her in a clear, arresting vision. He asked her to start painting holy icons. He spoke to her in a commanding manner.

Mother Stavritsa had never painted icons or received instruction in the art of painting. However,

---

[1] *Karyés, ho Lóphos ton Hagíon*, Athens, 1998, p. 271.

she felt sure that Raphael, being a saint, being wise, could not have asked her to do something impossible. She also recalled that the Holy Spirit rendered wise illiterate fishermen and gave them the gift of speaking in languages in which they had received no instruction. So she went and bought artists' brushes and paints, prayed ardently to receive the gift of painting holy icons, and started doing icons. She used as models some photographs she had of icons painted by Kontoglou and of works done at the Holy Mountain of Athos, and put to use everything she could recall of the technique that was used by Kontoglou, whom she had watched doing panel icons.

Her progress was rapid. In 1963 she did several excellent icons, with the intention of giving them to the Convent of St. Raphael as gifts. One of them depicted Christ; two, the Theotokos; a fourth, the Martyrs of Thermi: Raphael, Nicholas, and Irene. Before taking them to the Convent, she went to Kontoglou's home and showed them to him for comment. He was quite impressed, he regarded them as very successful. They are to be seen to this day in both the ground-floor church, which is dedicated to the Martyrs and where their relics are kept, and also in the upper church.

Mother Stavritsa regarded her skill as an icon painter as something God-given, to be used especially as an important means of teaching the Orthodox Christian Faith. St. John Damascene (eighth century) and other holy Fathers of the Church emphasize the function that holy icons serve of teaching the Faith. He likens them to books. Thus, he says: "What the book is to the literate, icons are to the illiterate, and what speech is to hearing, that the icon is to sight. Books and speech teach by means of words, while icons teach by means of forms and colors." And St. Basil the Great (fourth century) remarks that "icons are the never-silent heralds of the honor that is due to holy personages.... They teach those who see them with a soundless voice."

As an iconographer, she followed Kontoglou's example of employing Byzantine archetypes, avoiding modernistic ones, and painting with the accompaniment of Byzantine chant. In one of her letters she says about the latter.

"During the time when I am painting icons, I listen to the psalmody of Archon Protopsaltis Harilaos Taliadoros of Thessaloniki recorded in cassettes. Such beautiful chanting! It lifts me up to Heaven. I believe it helps me make icons that are beautiful, alive, stirring."

Kontoglou did not listen to Byzantine music recorded on reels or cassettes, but did the chanting himself, for he was proficient in this sacred art.

The Life of Mother Stavritsa

Blessed Mother Stavritsa viewed both the *monastic way* and the *missionary way* as leading to the same goal, to *theosis*, to everlasting-union with God, which constitutes salvation.[1] And she had what the Greek Church Fathers call "*klísis meióta*," that is, sheer *inclination*, for *both*. What was decisive in her choice between the two paths was what the Fathers call "*klésis me éta*," which means a call from God. This she received in very vivid form. Among the biographical notes which she left are the following:

"I am a simple woman. Do not think that I am important. I am a simple woman who from the time I was a little girl have believed in God.

"One night in 1969, during the Great Lent, I felt a hand which pulled me vigorously while I was sleeping. It lifted me up and I saw before me Christ. I stood quite astonished by this miracle of seeing the Lord before me, because I was also afraid. I have heard that Christ never appears alive before anyone.

"He told me: 'Go and help the uncivilized in Africa.' He pointed with His finger and I saw as in a movie views of all of the places and cities of Africa which I later visited. When I turned my head, He vanished.

---

[1] Regarding the paths that lead to salvation see my book *Paths and Means to Holiness*, Etna, California, 1986.

"Then I handled my shoulders. Am I alive, I asked? My soul answered: 'Yes, you are alive.' Was it perhaps an illusion, due to mental derangement, or a dream? 'Stavritsa,' replied my soul, commanding me: 'Stavritsa, kneel down, it was Christ, Who calls you to go to the uncivilized peoples of Africa.' Then I replied, mentally: 'I shall come, my Lord. I shall leave my son, my daughter-in-law, my grandchildren. I detach myself from everything: my possessions, my job, and I come. I shall try to prepare myself now and come promptly.' And this is what I did, my brethren.

"What I am telling you is the truth, believe it. All things can be done, because for God everything is possible. Earlier, I had entreated God to help me become an icon painter in order to make holy icons for the Church of Saint Raphael in Lesvos, those of the iconostasis. They were done successfully. And I have done many other icons that are scattered in various churches of Kenya and elsewhere in Africa."[1]

Heeding the call of God to become a missionary in Africa, Stavritsa left America and went and worked as a missionary in a number of African countries, especially Kenya, Uganda, and Zaire. Her missionary activities began in Kenya, continued in Zaire, then in

---

[1] From the periodical *Ho Poimén* ("The Shepherd"), Mytilene, February 2000, pp. 57-58.

Uganda, and again in Kenya. They extended over a period of thirty years.

Her God-pleasing deeds in Africa are innumerable and of a quite significant nature. An account of them up to the year 1988 is given in a typewritten "Testimony" (as it is headed) written in English and dated March 4, 1988. The document begins with the following statements:

"This is a presentation of my missionary tasks and endeavors which I undertook after I heard the calling from our Lord Jesus Christ, appealing and addressing His words to each one of us who is a member of the One, Holy, Universal, and Apostolic Church, our Orthodox Church, the words: 'Go and preach the Gospel.'[1]

"Without our Lord's blessing nothing can be accomplished. So I attribute everything to Him and Him alone.

"Being the least one of His servants, I, Stavritsa, worked and continue to work for His Glory by building churches in missionary Africa, by painting holy icons to beautify God's Houses, by providing holy coverings, vestments, landscaping, and many other needs that any such facility requires, such as guestrooms and houses,

---

[1] Mark 16.15.

so that there would be a home for gathering the faithful for catechism, study, conferences. I was the 'nurse' and the 'doctor' for the people also.

"I shall begin my account by speaking about the building or completion of churches in different parts of Africa, where Orthodoxy is taking root. I shall try to recall and record all my works and deeds in chronological order."

Mother Stavritsa goes on to list the churches which she either built from the foundations up, or whose construction she completed, or whose foundation she laid, or whose interior she furnished with panel icons done by her hand, sacred vessels, and so on. Her list proceeds in chronological order, beginning with the churches in Kenya from the year 1969 on, as follows:

1. *Saint Paul's Church* at Kagira (Waithaka). Mother Stavritsa painted all the panel icons, beautifying the church.

2. *Church of the All-Holy Virgin Mary* at Ngecha. Stavritsa contributed to the completion of the church, both by providing materials and by physical labor. Under her supervision and direction the landscaping around the church was completed. She supplied the sacred vessels, and also put a fence around the property for protecting it.

3. *Church of Saints Raphael, Nicholas, and Irene* at Thogoto. She laid the foundation of the edifice, completed its construction, and provided landscaping with lovely beds of flowers on the grounds to beautify the church's surroundings. In addition, she provided the sacred vessels as well as all the furnishings needed for the church, including the holy icons.

4. *Saints Luke's Church* at Nyathuna. She completed the construction of the church, furnished it with icons on the iconostasis, provided the sacred vessels, chandeliers, etc., and had the property duly fenced.

5. *Saint John the Theologian's Church* at Kahuho. She completed the construction of the church and furnished it with icons on the iconostasis and with everything needed for serving the faithful. She also provided the necessary fencing.

6. *Saint Panteleimon's Church* at Kerwa. She completed the construction of the church, did all the iconography, and bought the holy vessels.

7. *Church of the Transfiguration of Our Savior* at Kanjeru. She completed the construction of the church, built of stones, and furnished it with icons, holy vessels, etc., fenced it around, and enhanced the church grounds with landscaping.

8. *Saint Nectarios of Aegina Church* at Gikambura. She helped to complete the construction of the edifice, fenced the grounds, landscaped them, supplying them with trees and flower beds. For the interior, she made icons and purchased holy vessels for the Church services.

9. *Saint Andrew's Church* at Kimengwa (Western Kenya). She constructed it from the foundation up, built of bricks, did all the iconography, and supplied it with everything necessary for its holy services.

10. *Saints Peter and Paul Church* at Ka-anja in Embu. She helped to finish the construction from the foundation up and supplied all the interior furnishings, including the icons of the iconostasis, and completed the landscaping, putting many trees and flowers of various kinds.

11. *Saint Michael the Archangel's Church* at Runyenje (Embu). She built this church from the foundation up and supplied it with interior furnishings, including holy vessels.

12. *Church of Saint Luke* at Kihuti in Nyeri. She helped to finish the construction, bought holy vessels, and decorated the edifice with holy icons.

13. *Saint Gabriel the Archangel's Church* at King'eero. She helped to finish this church, made of timber, and supplied all the interior furnishings.

14. *Saint Iakovos' Church* at Nyanduma. She completed the construction of this wooden church and did the icons for it.

15. *Saint Nicholas' Church* at Elburgon (Nakuru). She laid the foundation of this church, but did not finish the construction of it.

(16. *Church of Saints Constantine and Helen*. This church is not listed in the above-mentioned document of 1988. In a letter to me dated August 26, 1994, Mother Stavritsa says that the Missionary Society of Thessaloniki gave her $4,000.00 to complete the construction of the Church of Saints Constantine and Helen in a town near Nairobi. She adds that she has begun purchasing the timber for the roof, and that she is going to buy the iconostasis and paints.)

(17. *Church of Saint Luke* at Nairobi. This is another church not listed in the above document, because it was built later. In the same letter, (August 26, 1994), Missionary Stavritsa informs me that the Metropolitan of Kavala Prokopios gave her $10,519.00 to begin the construction of a Church dedicated to the Apostle Luke, at an unspecified place in Kenya. I have no information as to the extent to which she succeeded in doing this.)

All the above-listed churches are in *Kenya*. The two that follow in Mother Stavritsa's 1988 list are in *Zaire*.

18. *Church of the Protomartyr Stephen* at Ruthigiti. She constructed the foundation of stones.

19. *Church of Saint John the Baptist* at Likasi. She built this church and its belfry, and supplied it with the necessary interior furnishings.

At Uganda, which borders on its east side with Kenya, Mother Stavritsa was not able to build a church, due to the fact that at the time when everything was ready for her to proceed with this undertaking a serious health problem arose, and she had to leave Uganda. An official document, dated March 26, 1994, written by Bishop Theodoros Nankyama of Uganda, contains the following:

"Missionary Mrs. Stavritsa Zachariou, our beloved Mother and spiritual friend of our Church, revisited Uganda between the 15th and 26th of March 1994. We were *all* very happy to receive her after a long time of absence. As usual, Missionary Mrs. Stavritsa Zachariou was very much concerned with the well-being of the Orthodox Clergy in Uganda. She donated to them the sum of five hundred ($500.00) United States dollars for sharing among *all* the twenty priests, in order to meet some of their personal needs.

The Life of Mother Stavritsa 115

"I wish to thank Missionary Stavritsa for this generous donation to my priests, and at the same time I pray for her good health and long life.

"I feel extremely sorry for Mama Stavritsa's not being able to carry out the construction of a church in Uganda due to the recent deterioration of her health. She obtained a doctor's recommendation to return to Nairobi immediately for an intensive medical examination."

The document has the heading: "Statement of Fact Regarding Missionary Mrs. Stavritsa Zachariou." It is signed by "Bishop Theodorous" (thus written), and has the seal of the Orthodox Church at Kampala, Uganda. Kampala is the capital of Uganda. Most of the Orthodox Ugandans live in that city.

Although she did not build a church in Uganda, Mother Stavritsa did icons for several churches there during earlier sojourns in that country. Writing to me on May 22, 1975, she mentioned her missionary activities in Uganda. With regard to iconography, she wrote that she painted icons in the traditional, Byzantine style, for the whole iconostasis of the Church of St. Nicholas at Kampala. Later, she did panel icons for other Orthodox Churches in Uganda.

Her part in the construction of the churches was that of an *architect* who designed their form, specified their dimensions, and provided the materials. It was also that of a *laborer*. In an article about her which appeared in the February 2000 issue of the periodical *Ho Poimén* of Mytilene, she is quoted as having once said that after a day spent in the construction of a church she returned home very tired:

"I had to oversee the workers, to go and buy the materials needed for building the churches, to watch for any mistakes they might make. The Lord illuminated me to detect any mistakes. At night, when I returned home, as soon as I opened the door I stretched out on my bed tired, dirty with cement and other materials. Often I fell asleep at once and woke up around three o'clock to cense the holy icons, to pray and thank the Lord for the day's activities."[1]

(When she was not thus exhausted, Mother Stavritsa was accustomed upon returning home to read the Vesper prayers, to have supper, and then to read the Apodeipnon prayers and the Salutations to the Theotokos; and around midnight to rise, take her prayer-rope and say mentally the Jesus Prayer.)

Her aspiration to build churches in Africa continued to be strong even in the last years of her earthly life. Thus, she is quoted as having said: "I am

---

[1] *Ho Poimén*, February, 2000, p. 59.

eighty years of age, and the time of my death is near. Perhaps I will live a few more years, as the Lord wills. I must continue to work as a missionary, painting icons, building another church where they have none. I want to erect another church as a beacon of Orthodoxy in the depths of Africa."[1]

The contribution of Blessed Stavritsa to Orthodox Missionary work in Africa was not restricted to painting icons for the churches and to building or completing churches. Parallel to these activities, and of great importance also, was spreading knowledge of the Orthodox Faith by means of the spoken word. In her "Testimony" which I mentioned earlier, she says:

"All the years that I served our Holy Church as a missionary, my primary responsibility, as I felt it, was preaching the Gospel. Jesus, I believe, needs persons to preach, in a *humble* and *simple* manner, His Word." In one of her letters she says that she told the congregation: "God sent me here from America twenty years ago to be close to you, because He loves you very much and wants you to receive the Gospel, to receive the light, to banish the darkness of idolatry and unbelief."

---

[1] *Ibid.*, p. 58.

Mother Stavritsa often spoke in the churches she built, as well as in others, at the end of the Divine Liturgy. She explained the significance of the Gospel excerpt that was read during the Liturgy, and answered questions regarding Orthodox worship and the Orthodox Faith in general. This she did during the whole period of thirty years as a missionary in Africa. She addressed specially the children, exhorting them to become good Orthodox Christians.

She spoke either in Greek or in English—according as the priest or some other person who was present knew the Greek or the English language and could translate what she said into the native tongue. Many priests in Uganda are fluent in Greek, having been educated in Greek schools in Alexandria or Greece, including the School of Theology of the University of Athens. This is probably true also of a good number of Orthodox priests in Kenya and Zaire.

With regard to the Greek language in Uganda, it is worth noting that in a letter which Mother Stavritsa sent me from Kampala, Uganda, dated September 10, 1974, she says that at the Forefeast of the Nativity of the Theotokos on September 7, the boys and the girls of the parish of St. Nicholas there chanted all the hymns and read all the Prophecies in the Greek language.

In some other letters she speaks of group Baptisms (*homadikaí Baptíseis*), and says that she catechizes such groups, using teachings of Holy Scripture from Adam and Eve to the Resurrection of our Lord. "We speak of the true God, His love for us, who forgave our sins and made us His children."

Her teaching of the true Faith was also effected by means of the icons which she painted for the churches, as well as by means of large numbers of icons in the form of color prints which she distributed. She also taught the Faith by means of numerous books which she gave away to literate individuals and to the library of the Orthodox Seminary at Nairobi. This Seminary was established by the late Archbishop of Cyprus Macarios. She ascribed considerable importance to that library and made special efforts to supply it with much needed books. In some of her letters she emphasized the need of books which explain in the English language the *differences* that separate the Orthodox Church from heterodox Christian Confessions. "It is a great necessity," she remarks in a letter dated December 16, 1989, "that our Orthodox brethren know these differences."

In the already referred to 1988 document, in which she describes her missionary activities in Africa,

Mother Stavritsa makes the following pertinent remarks in the Epilogue:

"I admire some foreign missionaries that come from abroad with their families, and live in this house, where I am going to spend the night. They are young couples with three to four children... Husbands and wives are medical doctors... They have some idea of our true faith, Orthodoxy. Up to 1050 all Christians were united, were Orthodox. All were doing the sign of the Cross in the same way, had the same Divine Liturgy, had the same Holy Tradition, the same Saints in all the churches. But this union was torn by the Pope due to his egotism. He instituted Baptism by sprinkling, instead of by immersion. He changed the Orthodox doctrine about the Holy Trinity and later that about the Holy Virgin Mary, asserting that she was born of the Holy Spirit and therefore is God. The Pope moved from one mistake to another, declaring, for instance, that he is infallible, whereas in truth only God is infallible, and he abolished many Saints of the Church.

The missionary activities of Blessed Mother Stavritsa also included teaching people how to cross themselves, how to fast, how to pray, in general, how to lead a true Christian life. They extended, further, to providing homes for priests who did not have any, offering them much needed financial assistance; giving to needy persons food and clothing; caring for the sick—both clergy and laity, both young and old—taking them to hospitals and providing them with medicines; teaching women sewing, making clothes, cooking, and general household management; and sending children and young men to Greece to get a general and theological education.

In order to achieve these things, Missionary Stavritsa collaborated with Greek and native bishops and priests, and also worked independently, according to the circumstances. Among the missionaries from Greece with whom she worked were Fathers Chrysostomos Papasarantopoulos. Athanasios Anthidis, Cosmas Gregoriatis (of the Monastery of Gregoriou of the Holy Mountain of Athos), and Amphilochios Tsoukos. She received much needed moral and material support from the Greek Missionary Society at Thessaloniki, from Archbishop Iakovos of America, from Metropolitan Silas of New Jersey, from Father Alexander Veronis of Lancaster, Pennsylvania, from various Greek-Orthodox parishes and philanthropic societies, and from many pious individuals, men and women.

Her great success as a missionary was due to all these factors and to her radiant virtues: her deep

Orthodox Christian faith and love, her benevolence, her kindness, her humility, her candidness, her courage, her purity, her prudence, her extraordinary resourcefulness and greatness of soul.

The missionary activities of Blessed Mother Stavritsa occasionally were interrupted by pilgrimages. She went again and again to the Convent of St. Raphael at Karyes, Lesvos, to pray and to venerate the relics of this great Martyr and his fellow Martyrs Nicholas and Irene and "receive their blessing," as she says in her letters. She went to the Convent of Evangelismos at Ainousa Island of Chios. She went to her native place, Kydoniai, and prayed at the surviving churches or their ruins. She went to Constantinople and visited the great Church of Hagia Sophia and all the other Orthodox Shrines and prayed there. She went to the island of Rhodes and spent a number of weeks at one of the convents, participating in the religious life of the nuns and painting icons.

Her longest period of rest from her arduous missionary activities in Africa took place during 1997-1998, at the town of Arnaia, the seat of the Metropolis of Hierissos, the Holy Mountain of Athos, and Ardameriou. She went there at the invitation of Metropolitan Nicodemos, whom she knew well, as he had served for many years as Chancellor of the Holy

The Life of Mother Stavritsa

Metropolis of Mytilene. Her life there was of a monastic type, with daily church services, private prayer and study at the guesthouse, and common meals. Her sojourn lasted about a year and a half. It was a pleasant, restful, and spiritually uplifting one. However, she felt very strongly that she should return to Africa to complete the construction of a church which she had undertaken to build and to continue teaching the Faith to the natives.

Now and then, from 1994 on, Mother Stavritsa encountered certain health problem. First there appeared a problem with the heart, then a fracture of the pelvis that resulted from a fall, and finally a cataract in one of her eyes. These were successfully treated at a Chicago hospital; and each time she returned to Africa to continue her missionary activities.

She reposed in the Lord at the age of 84 while at her place of residence in Nairobi. Archimandrite Chrysostomos Maidonis, Chancellor of the Holy Metropolis of Ierissos, the Holy Mountain and Ardameriou, has written about her repose: "She left her last breath at Nairobi on January 3, 2000. It was 8 o'clock in the morning, after her morning prayers and as she was getting ready to resume her activities. Her Guardian Angel took her soul and led it to the Lord that she might rest eternally near Him. And now her body rests in the African soil, near the relics of other holy missionaries of Orthodoxy: Chrysostomos Papasarantopoulos, Cosmas Gregoriatis, Hariton Pneumatikakis, and others."[1]

Blessed Mother Stavritsa worked as a missionary in Africa longer than any other Orthodox missionary there. She was dearly loved by thousands of Orthodox Africans in Kenya, Uganda, and Zaire, to whom she was known as "Mama Stavritsa." They were all deeply saddened by her death, for she was for them a very lovable holy woman.

That is the way she was regarded by all who knew her well personally. Thus, Metropolitan Silas of New Jersey, who had been entrusted by Archbishop Iakovos with handling the correspondence of the Archdiocese of America with Mother Stavritsa addressed her in the correspondence as *Hosiotáte* Kyria Stavritsa Zachariou ("Most Holy Mrs. Stavritsa Zachariou"). And in a letter to her dated January 11, 1991, he says:

"I follow mentally your activities and pray for you and your work. I am aware of the difficulties and

---

[1] *Mía Synchrone Hierapóstolos, Stavrítsa Zacharíou* ("A Contemporary Missionary, Stavritsa Zachariou") periodical *Exoteriké Hierapostolé*, January-March, 2000, p. 54. Papasarantopoulos died in 1972; Cosmas, in 1989; Hariton, in 1997.

adversities which you encounter, but I believe in the power of your inward faith and foresee the victory.

"You think that you are in Africa because you desire it. I believe that you have a call from Christ. You are there in order to transmit the Orthodox Christian Faith and to testify to its glory, its history, and the richness of its spirituality. You are under Divine protection, as is proven by the incidents which you mention. You are not frightened by your being in lands unknown to you, and you are not stopped by the lack of material means, or by the negative reactions of those who are far from Christ and His Law.

"You are writing history for Orthodoxy's Missionary Activity. The descendants of our African Orthodox brethren will hear about your missionary work with admiration and joy."

A great deal may well be expected to be written about Blessed Mother Stavritsa Zachariou in the years ahead, extolling her contributions as a missionary in Africa, describing in greater detail than I have done her holy life, character, and thought, and writing encomia about them.

GREEK ORThODOX ARChDIOCESE OF NORTh AND SOUTh AMERICA
ΕΛΛΗΝΙΚΗ ΟΡΘΟΔΟΞΟΣ ΑΡΧΙΕΠΙΣΚΟΠΗ ΒΟΡΕΙΟΥ & ΝΟΤΙΟΥ ΑΜΕΡΙΚΗΣ

10 EAST 79th STREET, NEW YORK, N.Y. 10021 • TEL (212) 570-3500 • CABLE. ARCHGREEK, NEW YORK

11ην Ἰανουαρίου, 1991

Ὁσιωτάτην Κυρία
Σταυρίτσα Ζαχαρίου
P.O.Box 74833
Nairobi, Kenya

Ὁσιωτάτη κα Σταυρίτσα, Ἱεραπόστολε,

Λαμβάνω τά γράμματά σας καί τά διαβάζω μέ πολύ ἐνδιαφέρον, χαράν καί ἀγαλλίασιν διότι δι᾽ αὐτῶν πληροφοροῦμαι τό ἐπιτελούμενον ὑφ᾽ ὑμῶν ἔργον Χριστοῦ.

Σᾶς παρακολουθῶ νοερῶς καί προσεύχομαι δι᾽ ὑμᾶς καί τό ἔργον σας. Γνωρίζω τάς δυσκολίας καί τίς ἀντιξόοτητες, ἀλλά πιστεύω εἰς τήν δύναμιν τῆς ἐσωτερικῆς σας πίστεως καί διαβλέπω τήν νίκην.

Νομίζετε ὅτι εὐρίσκεσθε εἰς τήν Ἀφρικήν ἐπειδή ἐσεῖς τό ἐπιθυμεῖτε; Ἐγώ πιστεύω ὅτι ἔχετε κλῆσιν Χριστοῦ. Εὑρίσκεσθε ἐκεῖ διά νά προβάλλετε τήν Ὀρθοδοξίαν καί νά μαρτυρήσετε τήν δόξαν της, τήν ἱστορίαν της καί τόν πλοῦτον τῆς θρησκευτικῆς της ζωῆς. Εὑρίσκεσθε ὑπό προστασία, ἀπόδειξις ἡ συμπεριφορά τοῦ Ἀφρικανοῦ ἀδελφοῦ μας, ὅταν εὑρέθητε εἰς τήν πόλιν του ἄνευ χρημάτων καί κατά συνέπειαν ἐγκαταλελειμμένη.

Μετά πολλῆς χαρᾶς καί ἱκανοποιήσεως παρακολουθῶ τό ἔργον σας, καί βλέπω ὅτι ἔχετε ἀποστολήν. Δέν σᾶς φοβίζει τό ἄγνωστον τοῦ τόπου, δέν σᾶς ἐμποδίζει ἡ ἔλλειψις τῶν ὑλικῶν μέσων καί δέν σᾶς σταματᾶ ἡ ἀντίδρασις τοῦ ἀνθρώπου πού εὑρίσκεται μακράν ἀπό τόν Χριστόν καί τόν νόμον του.

Γράφετε ἱστορίαν διά τήν Ὀρθόδοξον Ἱεραποστολήν, τήν ὁποίαν μετά θαυμασμοῦ καί ἀγαλλιάσεως θά πληροφοροῦνται, ἀπό αἰῶνες οἱ ἀπόγονοι τῶν ἀδελφῶν μας Ὀρθοδόξων Ἀφρικανῶν.

Διά τήν δράσιν σας, διά τήν προσφοράν σας, διά τάς προσωπικάς σας θυσίας σᾶς μακαρίζω καί σᾶς εὐχαριστῶ, ἐκ μέρους τῶν πολλῶν ἐδῶ θαυμαστῶν σας καί φίλων σας.

Σᾶς εὔχομαι ὁ καινούριος χρόνος νά ἀποβῆ γιά σᾶς καί τό πνευματικό σας ἔργον πρόξενος παντός ἀγαθοῦ καί καλοῦ.

Μετά πατρικῶν εὐχῶν καί ἀγάπης ἐν Κυρίῳ
Ὁ Μητροπολίτης,

Ὁ Νέας Ἱερσέης Σίλας

METROPOLITAN SILAS' LETTER
(A much reduced photocopy.)

Chapter 3

HOMILY ON THE FEAST OF HOLY THEOPHANY[1]

By Mother Stavritsa

Reverend Father Nicholas, I thank you for having invited me to come to your beautiful church, and given me the opportunity of attending the very beautiful and contrition-evoking Divine Liturgy, and praying together with this pious congregation.

Today, my brethren, God revealed to us the Holy Trinity. At the Jordan River there appeared a young man named John. He led an ascetic life. His food consisted only of wild honey and the tender shoots of herbs. He confessed multitudes who went to see him and to listen to his divinely inspired sermons. His garment was made of camel's hair, and he had a leathern girdle about his waist.

---

[1] Delivered in the Church of St. Luke the Evangelist at the town of Nyathuna in Kenya on January 6, 1993.

He told them to prepare the way of the Lord. Another one is coming after me, he said, whose sandals I am not worthy to unloose. He confessed the crowds and baptized them in the waters of the Jordan. And he said: "I am now baptizing you with water, but He Who will come will baptize you with the Holy Spirit, in the name of the Holy Trinity. Prepare yourselves to be ready to receive Him."[1]

One day our sweet John the Baptist and Prophet saw a certain young man full of goodness and spiritual magnificence, Who told Him: "John, I want you to baptize me." It was our Lord Jesus Christ at the age of thirty. John was astonished. "Lord," he said, "I need to be baptized by You. I am not worthy of performing this Mysterion.

"John," replied Christ, in a commanding manner, "You must baptize me!"

And our sinless Lord went into the waters of the Jordan. But what a great miracle took place at that moment! Heaven opened and there was heard the voice of God saying: "This is my beloved Son, in Whom I am well pleased, listen to Him."[2] And immediately the Spirit of God descended like a dove and lighted on Jesus.

---

[1] Matthew 3:11, Mark 1:3.
[2] Matthew 3:17; 17:5.

On the Feast of Holy Epiphany

Now on this day, my brethren, there was revealed to us the Holy Trinity by God our heavenly Father. My beloved brethren, let your minds take flight for a moment and go to the Jordan River—where I have gone in actuality twice—and see the face of our Lord in the waters, into which He immersed Himself three times. Who? The Son of God Who was born of the Evervirgin Mary in the form of man. Think of the astonishment of St. John, to be esteemed worthy of baptizing our Lord and of placing his right hand on His head!

Let your mind, my dear brethren, think of the infinite love of the Heavenly Father for us, to send His only-begotten Son to teach for three years, ever doing the will of His Father.

Reflect, also, on the fact that despite all this, the wickedness of some men to place their great Benefactor on the Cross—Him Who gave sight to the blind, healed the lepers, raised dead persons, and taught love and the equality of all men! He gave His blood for the salvation of mankind. He opened the gates of Paradise, so that we might enter into the Kingdom of God, where there is no sorrow or groaning, but only unending life of blessedness.

The four Evangelists wrote the Gospels. They described what their eyes saw and what their ears

CHRIST
Icon by Mother Stavritsa. 1968.

heard. And we have these as the greatest treasure in our homes. Every home should have the Book of the Gospels. You should read it every day. And you should have your children listen.

Mothers should teach their children, from an early age on, to love God before everything else.

I entreat you, my dear brethren, to remember in your prayers me the least of women, who am now here close to you. I wish you many blessed years.

I thank all of you, especially Father Nicholas. May all of you have the blessing of the Holy Trinity.

Chapter 4

OUR SAINTS[1]

By Mother Stavritsa

The Saints received Divine grace due to their sacrifices for the Lord. They received the Holy Spirit, and that is why they perform miracles. God hears them and the miracles take place immediately. The Saints whose bodies were buried a few years after the Resurrection of our Lord listen to us. The same is true of the Saints who came after them.

In our time, the Saints of Thermi in Lesvos—Raphael, Nicholas, and Irene—have appeared many times. Even I who am not worthy saw them on Great Thursday of 1963. At that time, I brought there the icons which I had painted as a gift to the ground-level church that had just been built, dedicated to these Saints. They appeared suddenly near an olive tree which shone at that moment. I was with two other women. We were overwhelmed with emotion! We cried! We prayed to them with fervor! They stayed

---

[1] Written in 1985, as part of the document entitled "Missionary Life in Africa."

there for a few moments, and we could see them clearly. After that there was darkness at that spot, and we could not see them.

We spent the whole night worshipping together with all the faithful until morning. We knelt before the icon of the Crucified Christ. What we were permitted to see that night I will never forget.

In Africa,[1] I built a beautiful Church of St. Raphael. A woman, who was the mother of six, was healed in that church; she had been suffering from cancer. Many other miracles have taken place in that church.

✻ ✻ ✻

Recently, I went to the Monastery of Sts. Raphael, Nicholas, and Irene. I lingered at the grave of St. Raphael and venerated his holy relics.

At 11:30 in the night, one of the nuns led me to the Abbess' Office (*Hegoumeneíon*) to sleep on a bench that was along the wall. There were no vacant beds in the guesthouse, I was told. She spread a sheet on the bench, placed a pillow, and departed. I stretched out on the bench to sleep. However, on the wall across from the bench was a large clock which produced loud noise, keeping me awake.

---

[1] In Thogoto, Kenya.

Soon, the door opened and a little girl with a longish dress entered into the room. She went and stretched out on the next bench along the wall. I spoke out and said: "That clock is not going to let me sleep."

In less than a minute the little girl said to me: "Aunt, aunt (*theía*), the clock has stopped." And the clock did stop.

"Yes," I said to her, "I noticed it, and I thank God and Saint Raphael for this."

Shortly after this, I decided that it was proper for me to rise and speak to the girl, asking her where she is from, and why she came to the Abbess' Office to sleep. Was there no bed for her in the guesthouse?

To my surprise, I saw that the little girl was not at the place where I had seen her recline. I opened the door and looked in all directions for a good while. But I could not see her anywhere. And there was great silence. At once I realized that the little girl whom I took to be from one of the villages was Saint Irene, who is shown in the icon flanked on either side by Saints Raphael and Nicholas. I glorified Saint Irene for the miracle which she had performed. At the same time, however, I felt sorry that I did not realize this earlier, when she said to me: "Aunt, aunt!" to go close to her, to try to embrace her, and to cry, recalling her martyrdom.

In the morning, I asked many persons, including those who had slept at the guesthouse. Nobody had seen the little girl."[1]

STS. RAPHAEL, NICHOLAS, AND IRENE

---

[1] The second text of this chapter is a translation which I have made from a two-page letter entitled *Pros Dóxan tou Theoú* ("For the Glory of God"), which I received from Mother Stavritsa towards the end of March 1991.

Chapter 5

BYZANTINE CHANT IN UGANDA[1]

By MOTHER STAVRITSA

A certain Roman Catholic lady with whom I had luncheon at the Missionary House at Kampala in Uganda, and is a native of Kampala, said to me that the Orthodox there have an excellent bishop, Theodoros Nankyama: "He makes religious speeches at the Radio and the Television Stations two or three times a week. He speaks so beautifully, and we look forward to hearing him during the scheduled hour. His choir is excellent."

Every Sunday the personnel of the Radio Station of Kampala transmits during a period of two hours the beautiful morning hymns of the Orthros, the Doxology, and part of the Divine Liturgy. The music used is the Byzantine. Under the supervision of Bishop Theodoros, the hymns have been translated from the

---

[1] An article entitled *Byzantinés Akolouthíes sten Ougánta* ("Byzantine Church Services in Uganda"), published in 1989 in the periodical of the Missionary Society of Thessaloniki.

Greek into the Ugandan language. He mastered the Greek language and the sacred art of Byzantine chant while a student at the School of Theology of the University of Athens.

This presentation of the Orthodox Church in Uganda is a result of the untiring efforts of Bishop Theodoros. No heterodox Church has the great treasures of Byzantine music.

Let all of us pray that God give him abundantly His grace and many years. Personally, I was greatly moved when I visited one afternoon his class and saw with what patience he taught Byzantine music to the youths, and I heard them chanting all the troparia and other Church hymns in their language but in conformity with the modes and melodies of Byzantine chant.

Chapter 6

SAYINGS OF MOTHER STAVRITSA

When we have Christian love and let the Grace of God direct us, it illuminates us and protects us from every evil.

※ ※ ※

All-good God saved me many times from knives, arrows, robbers, snakes, lions, and so on. I glorify Him with all my soul. I set my hope on God and entreat Him that I be always in His hands, in order to work for Him until late old age.

※ ※ ※

Paradise is not won by leading a soft life. There is need of privations, efforts, afflictions, trials.

※ ※ ※

Our sweet Jesus Christ does not want mercenaries. He wants genuine strugglers.

※ ※ ※

He tests His chosen ones during this brief life. Christians are wise when they see all things in proper perspective and accept the afflictions that befall them as promptings for self-improvement.

***

Our holy Fathers fought in defense of our precious Orthodox Faith not with guns, but through their holy life, their faith in God, their saintliness. Similarly, we today must become good guards of the Faith. We must not let the heretics, wolves disguised as sheep, demolish the fortress of Orthodoxy.

***

With God's help, everything is possible. The Holy Spirit rendered wise the illiterate fishermen, and taught them languages, and they stirred the multitudes that followed them.

***

Do not let the so-called Jehovah's Witnesses enter into your homes. They are lying when they say that they accept the teachings of the Gospels. They are enemies of our Lord Jesus Christ and the Panagia, they do not believe in the Holy Trinity.

***

In Greece, unfortunately, the governments have let these persecutors of Christ penetrate into the country. They have instituted laws that exempt Jehovah's Witnesses from military service, and they otherwise pamper them.

***

Our Orthodox Church is the oldest Church, the One, genuine, Apostolic and Universal (*Katholiké*) Church.

***

What is the duty of us Orthodox Christians towards those who have the desire to become acquainted with our Faith? Must we not help them as much as possible to be saved? It is not right for us to remain inactive, while others proselytize. Should we turn our back to those who thirst to learn about the Orthodox religion? Then we shall be accountable to the Righteous Judge, Who gave us the talent of teaching this Faith and enlightening others about it, whereas we keep it only for ourselves, turning a deaf ear to them.[1]

***

I think particularly of Greek immigrants. Why do not some of our people become active in missionary work? Why is it that their mind is always directed to becoming rich? We have the wealth of the true religion. What other wealth do we need?

***

People say many and various things about me. However, I perform my duty, reflecting on the fact that

---

[1] Cf. the Parable of the talents, Matthew, Chapter 25.

our Lord Jesus Christ lifted me with His hand from my bed while I was sleeping, telling me: "Go and help the people of Africa."

※ ※ ※

The mind of the true Christian must always be directed to the eternal life. He must not be overcome by the love of money. He must be satisfied if he has enough for the necessities of life, trusting fully that God will not abandon him. This has been proven a great many times. We must *not* put our trust in the corruptible *body*, but must have our attention turned instead to our *soul*, so that it might one day stand before the throne of God and hear: "Well done, thou good and faithful servant: thou hast been faithful over few things, I will make thee ruler over many things: enter thou into the joy of the Lord."

APOLYTIKION

Plagal of the Fourth Mode.

In thee the image was preserved
with exactness, O Mother;
For taking up thy cross,
thou didst follow Christ,
and by thy deeds thou didst teach us
to overlook the flesh,
for it passeth away,
but to attend to the soul,
since it is immortal.
Wherefore, O righteous Stavritsa,
thy spirit rejoiceth with the Angels.

BIBLIOGRAPHY

Cavarnos, Constantine, *Meetings with Kontoglou*. Belmont, Massachusetts, 1992.

Cavarnos, Constantine, "Mother Stavritsa Zachariou, Missionary in Africa," in *The Hellenic Chronicle* (Boston), May 3, 10, 24, 31—2000.

Koukliatis, Georgios, theologian, "*Éphyge he 'Máma' Stavrítsa*" ("Mama Stavritsa has Departed"), in *Hágios Kosmás Aitolós* ("Saint Cosmas Aitolos"), Quarterly Periodical of Orthodox External Missions, Thessaloniki, January-March, 2000, pp. 255-258.

Koukliatis, Georgios, "*Stavrítsa Zacharíou, Hierapóstolos,* in *Exoteriké Hierapostolé* ("External Missions"), Quarterly Periodical of the Orthodox Missionary Brotherhood of Thessaloniki, January-March, 2000, pp. 57-65.

Maidonis, Chrysostomos, Archimandrite, "*Mia Synchronos Hierapóstolos, Stavrítsa Zacharíou*" ("A Contemporary Missionary, Stavritsa Zachariou"), in *Exoteriké Hierapostolé*, January-March, 2000, pp. 53-56.

Ralli, Vasiliki, *Karyés, ho Lóphos ton Hagíon* ("Karyes, the Hill of the Saints"), Athens, 1998.

The Life of Mother Stavritsa

Soteriou, Georgios P., theologian, "*Stavritsa Zachariou, Hierapóstolos* ("Stavritsa Zachariou, Missionary"), in *Ho Poimén* ("The Shepherd"), monthly periodical of the Holy Metropolis of Mytilene, February, 2000, pp. 57-59.

Stavritsa Zachariou, *Presentation of My Missionary Tasks and Endeavors*. An eight-page typescript which describes chiefly her construction or completion in various ways of churches in Africa. The typing is single-spaced.

Stavritsa Zachariou, *A Journey from Nairobi, Kenya, to Lumumbasi, Zaire, through Tanzania, in 1985*. A six-page, single-spaced typescript, in which are described in a vivid manner the difficulties, the trials, the afflictions, and the dangers she encountered on the way, as well as the experience of God's protecting grace. The closing part is comprised of noteworthy remarks on missionary activity, on the Schism which began in the eleventh century, and on Saints.

Stavritsa Zachariou, 30 *Letters*, and about 70 *Photographs* with explanations and comments, dating from 1971 to 1999.

EPILOGUE

*W*ith the present volume I bring to a close the series *Modern Orthodox Saints*. This series is the result of a sustained effort to make better known to members of the Orthodox Christian Church, and to others as well, the beautiful and inspiring life, character, and thought of holy personages of the last two and a half centuries. The response to this effort has been most heartening. Orders for the volumes of the series have been coming regularly from private individuals, from schools of theology for classroom use, from Orthodox Church parish libraries and bookstores, as well as from many other kinds of libraries and bookstores. Among libraries of schools of theology that have all the volumes of this series are Andover-Harvard Theology Library, Yale Divinity School Library, Pitts Theology Library of Emory University, Speer Library of Princeton Theological Seminary, Graduate Theological Union Library at Berkeley California, Perkins Library of Duke University, Holy Cross Greek Orthodox School of Theology/Hellenic College Library, St. Vladimir's Seminary Library, St. Tikhon' Seminary Library, Holy Trinity Monastery Library (at Jordan-

Epilogue

ville, NY) and others. These libraries have the whole series.

My reason for deciding to stop the series with this, the 14th volume, is not due to a slackening of interest in *Modern Orthodox Saints* by the general reading-public, or by churches, or by academic institutions. Neither is it due to the absence of outstanding holy figures of the Orthodox Church besides those already presented in the series. With regard to the last point, it may be pointed out that during the last decade the Oecumenical Patriarchate of Constantinople officially recognized as Saints Father Papa-Nicholas Planas of Athens (1851-1932) and Archimandrite Anthimos (1869-1960), founder of the Convent Panagia Boetheia in Chios. Also to be noted is the fact that a number of recently reposed holy men are highly regarded by many, particularly Elder Hieronymos of Aegina (1883-1966), and Archimandrite Justin Popovich (1894-1979) of Serbia. My reason for not continuing to produce other volumes of the series *Modern Orthodox Saints* is that I have set for myself other important literary tasks which require all my time and energy as a writer.

INDEX OF PROPER NAMES

Agapios Landos, xvii, 56
Amphilochios Tsoukos, Father, 121
Andrew the "Fool" for Christ, St., 77
Anthidis, Athanasios, Father, 121
Antony the Great, St., 77, 78
Arsenios the Great, St., 77
Arsenios the New, St., viii-ix
Athanasios Parios, St., *see* Parios
Athenagoras, I, Patriarch, 35-36

Basil the Great, St., xviii, 106
Batistatos, Dionysios, 71-72
Bellos, Konstantinos, 35
Berdyaev, Nicholas, xvii
Bougatsos, N. Th., 71

Clement of Rome, St., xvii
Cosmas Gregoriatis, Father, 121, 124

Dorotheos, Abba, 74, 75
Doukakis, Konstantinos, 49

Elias the Prophet, 23, 37
Ephraim, Archimandrite, 45, 47, 52-53, 63ff., 73, 91
Ephraim the Syrian, St., xvii, 57

Gabriel Dionysiatis, Abbot, x, 71
Gerasimos of Kephallenia, St. 56
Gerostergios, Asterios, Father, 98
Gregory the Sinaite, St., 50-51
Hariton Pneumatikakis, Father, 124

Index of Proper Names

Helen, St., 98, 113

Iakovos, Archbishop of America, 121, 124
Iakovos of Epiros, Elder, vii-ix, 19-42
Irene, Martyr, of Thermi, Lesvos, 133-134
Isaac the Syrian, St., 74, 75, 77, 78

John Climacos, St., xvii, 87
John Damascene, St., 106
John the Baptist and Forerunner, 127-129
Joseph the Elder, the Hesychast, ix-x, 43-92
Joseph the Younger, of Cyprus, 60, 64, 65, 67, 91, 92

Kallinikos, Konstantinos N., Father, 26
Kontoglou, Photios, xi, xv, xvii, 23, 96, 101-103, 105, 106
Koukliatis, Georgios, 142

Kyrlis, Demetrios, 100

Landos, Agapios, *see* Agapios
Lukas of Sterion, Hosios, 77, 78

Macarios, Archbishop of Cyprus, 119
Macarios the Egyptian, the Great, St., 74, 75, 77-78
Maidonis, Chrysostomos, Archimandrite, 123, 142
Mantzaridis, Georgios I., 69
Mary the Egyptian, St., 78
Matthaiou, Victor, 49
Michael, Archbishop of America, 96
Michael the Archangel, 112

Nectarios of Aegina, St., 25-26, 78

Nicholas, Martyr, of Thermi, Lesvos, *see* Thermi
Nicodemos, Metropolitan of Hierissos, etc., 122
Nikephoros the Solitary, St., 50-51

Onouphrios the Athonite, St., 78

Palladios, 71
Panteleimon, Archimandrite, 72, 97, 98
Panteleimon, St., 111
Papademetriou, Alexandeos, 45
Papasarantopoulos, Chrysostomos, Father, 121, 124
Parios, Athanasios, St., 55
Paul the Apostle, 32, 76, 110, 12
Peter the Apostle, 112
Peter the Athonite, St., 78
Philaretos, Hermit of the Holy Mountain, xii

Pneumatikakis, Hariton, Father, 113

Ralli, Vasiliki, 104, 142
Raphael, Martyr, of Thermi, Lesvos, xvi, 103-104, 105, 122, 131, 132, 134

Schoinas, Soterios N., ix, xv, 61-63
Silas, Metropolitan of New Jersey, xvi, 121, 124
Stephen the Protomartyr, 114
Symeon the New Theologian, St., 48

Taliadoros, Harilaos, Protopsaltis, 106
Theodoros Nankyama, Bishop, 114-115, 135-136
Tsoukos, Amphilochios, Father, 121

Vasilopoulos, Haralampos, Archimandrite,

Index of Proper Names

vii, viii, xv, 21-23, 27, 35, 38
Veronis, Alexander, Father, 121

Vryenni, Abbess, 71

Zervakos, Philotheos, Archimandrite, xii

INDEX OF SUBJECTS

afflictions, 137
Africa, 97ff., 107, 132
Ainousa Island, Chios, 122
Aivalí, 100
America, 65, 102, 104
Anchored in God, 57, 73, 77, 91
angels, 51, 75, 89, 141
anger, 76, 80, 81
Apódeipnon, 34, 52, 116
arrogance, 86
Asia Minor, 100
askesis, 27, 37, 69
Athens, 36, 45, 55, 101, 136
Athos, Mount, 25, 27-28, 34,-35, 45ff., 56-57, 63
attention, 32,-33, 37, 40, 77; inner, 50-51, 58, 82

Baptism, 119, 120, 128
body, 85, 87, 140, 141
books, 97, 102-103, 119
Byzantine chant, 106-107, 135-136
Byzantine iconography, 96, 97, 101-102, 106, 115
Byzantine mystics, 50

Canada, 65
cancer, miraculous cure of, 132
candidness, 122
care of the soul, 88
cares, worldly, 49
catechism, 26, 110
chastity, 84, 85
Chios, 122
Christ, 30. 49, 61, 75, 76, 77, 83, 85, 86, 87, 107-109, 117, 125, 128, 131, 137, 138, 139
Church of
  St. Andrew at Kimengwa, Kenya, 112
  Sts. Constantine and Helen in Kenya, 113

150

Index of Subjects

St. Gabriel the Archangel at King'eero, 112
St. Iakovos at Nyathuna, Kenya, 113
St. John the Baptist at Likasi, Zaire, 114
St. John the Theologian in Kenya, 111
St. Luke at Kihuti in Nyeri, Kenya, 112
St. Luke at Nairobi, Kenya, 113
St. Luke at Nyathuna, Kenya, 111
St. Michael the Archangel at Runyenje (Embu), Kenya, 112
St. Nectarios of Aegina at Gikambura, Kenya, 112
St. Nicholas at Elburgon (Nakuru), Kenya, 113
St. Panteleimon at Kerwa, Kenya, 111
St. Paul in Kenya, 110
Sts. Peter and Paul, at Ka-anja, Kenya, 112
Sts. Raphael, Nicholas, and Irene in Kenya, 111
St. Stephen the Protomartyr at Ruthigiti, Zaire, 114
the Transfiguration of Our Savior at Kanjeru, Kenya, 111
the All-Holy Virgin Mary in Kenya, 110
Chruch unity, 120
Commandments, Divine, 28, 75, 86, 87
Communion, *see* Holy Communion
Confession, 27, 29-30, 35-36, 38, 39, 47, 55, 64, 80-81, 103, 122
Constantinople, 25-26, 35-36, 38, 41, 55, 103, 122
counseling, 31, 54, 61, 71, 85
courage, 80-81, 84, 85, 122

Desert Fathers and
  Mothers, 72, 74, 75,
  81
despair, 80
despondency, 80-81, 85
Devil, 31, 40, 80, 81
diet, 78
discernment, 84
distractious, 99
Divine grace, 35, 58, 79,
  80, 82
Divine Liturgy, 31, 32,
  34, 40, 52, 61, 118,
  120, 135

empirical verification, 50,
  56-57
Epiros, 23, 28, 37
error, 84
eternal life, 140
Evergetinos, 74, 75-76
evil, 51, 77, 84, 96, 137
experience, inner, 50-51
extremes, 86

faith, 31, 47, 75, 78, 84,
  119, 122, 125, 138,
  139
false belief, 84

fasting, 27, 33, 37, 82, 86,
  120
feelings, 31, 47, 75, 78
foreknowledge, 61, 63

gentleness, 84, 85-86
God, 21, 23, 27, 28, 33,
  37, 39, 40, 51, 54, 55,
  78, 82, 85, 86, 87, 107,
  119, 127, 128-130,
  131, 137, 138
Gospels, the, 31, 47, 117,
  118, 129-130, 138
grace, Divine, 33, 58, 78,
  82-86, 137
guarding of the senses, 82
guide, spiritual, 50, 57,
  78, 86

Halki School of Theol-
  ogy, 36
happiness, 51
hardships, 76, 81, 86-87
health, physical, 78, 86
  spiritual, 48, 82
heart, 50. 77
Hell, 82
heresy, 84, 137-138
hesychasts, 59, 60, 78

Index of Subjects

holiness, xvii, 21, 22, 27, 138
Holy Communion, 27, 31-32, 34, 39-40, 61, 82
Holy Mountain, *see* Athos
Holy Scriptures, 48, 74-75, 129-130
hope, 137
humility, 21-22, 29, 37, 47, 58, 79, 80, 81, 117, 122

icons, 95-98, 101-102, 104-106, 109-113, 117, 119
idolatry, 117
ignorance, 84
illumination, 83, 84
"image of God," 83-84, 89
immortality, 88, 140, 141
indolence, 85
interior prayer, *see* mental prayer
Ioannina, 24, 29-30, 35-36

Irene, St. of Thermi Lesvos, 132-134

Jeovah's Witnesses, 138
Jesus Prayer, 31, 39, 49-50, 82, 116
joy, 51, 85
Judgment, 82

Kalokairiné, 56-57
Kampala, 115, 118, 135
Karyes, Lesvos, 102, 103, 131ff.
Kenya, 98, 108-114, 124, 132, 142
kindness, 122
Kingdom of God, 36, 37, 76, 81, 129
knowledge, 83, 84
"Know thyself," 79, 84
Kydoníai (Aivalí), 100, 101, 102, 122

Ladder of Divine Ascent, 87
Lausiac History, 71
Lesvos, 100, 108, 122, 131; *see also* Mytilene
light, spiritual, 35, 60

"likeness of God," 83-84
Liturgical books, 34
Liturgy, *see* Divine
   Liturgy
lives of saints, 17, 49, 56,
   72, 74, 76, 81
love, 37, 51, 54, 58, 60,
   75, 76, 77, 81, 83, 84,
   86-87, 119, 122, 129,
   130, 137
lust, 80, 81
lying, 48

meditation, 36, 40, 82
Megas Synaxaristes, 49
mental prayer, ix, 31, 46,
   49, 51-52, 58, 59, 60,
   61, 77, 82
mind, 32, 33, 37, 40, 50,
   60, 82, 83, 140
miracles, 22-23, 28, 32-
   33, 35, 36, 37, 56-57,
   102-103, 107, 131
missionary, way, the, 107
moderation, 86
Monastery of
   Evangelismos at
   Oinousa, Island, 122

Monastery of St. Paul at
   Mount Athos, 45
Monastery of Philotheou
   at Mount Athos, 64-65,
   67
Monastery of St. Raphael
   at Lesvos, 102ff.
Monastery of the Prophet
   Elias in Epiros, 29, 37
Monastery of Vatopedi at
   Mount Athos, 64
monastic way, the, 29,
   107
Monastic Wisdom, 67, 71,
   73-89
Monodendrian, Epiros,
   23, 29, 37
mystics, 50, 52, 59, 60
Mytilenes, 100, 101, 122-
   123

Nairobi, 98, 119, 123,
   143
Nea Skete, 45ff., 57, 64
New Testamernt, 48, 75,
   119
Nicholas, St., of Thermi,
   Lesvos, *see* Thermi

Index of Subjects

obedience, 84, 86
Old Testament, 47-48, 75, 119
otherworldliness, 88

Paradise, 37, 82, 129, 137
Paros, Island of, 55
passionlessness, 79, 83
passions, 79-83, 86, 88
patience, 84, 85
Patriarchate of Constantinople, 35-36, 38, 41, 55
peace, inner, 51, 82, 85, 88
perfection, spiritual, 79, 83-84, 88
Philokalia, 51, 74
pilgrimages, 122, 129
prayer, 26, 27, 29, 31-34, 37-38, 49, 76, 81, 82, 120
Prayer-rope, 51
preaching, 26, 117
pride, 80, 84
priests, 29, 40, 41
privation, 29, 36, 137
prudence, 122
Psalms, 47

purification, 47, 50, 58, 81, 82, 86 88
purity, 79, 85, 122

reason, 81, 84
reading, 49-50, 74-77, 81
relics, sacred, 104, 105, 132
Repentance, 30, 38, 82
revelation, 51
Rhodes, 122

sainthood, 21, 35
saints, xvii, 21-23, 52, 55, 63, 74, 76, 89, 120, 143
Saluitations to the Theotokos, 75, 77, 116
salvation, 107, 129, 139
sanity, 49-50, 80-81
Satan, 31, 40, 80
Sayings of the Desert Fathers, 74
Schism, the, 120, 143
self-examination, 79
self-knowledge, 79, 84
senses, 82, 87
sermons, 26-27, 31

sin, 23, 30, 31, 33, 37, 40, 80, 82, 119
sloth, 80-81
soul, 30, 77, 81-82, 84, 88, 140
spiritual guide, 46, 50, 54, 57, 64, 74, 78-79, 86
spirituality, 34, 74, 83ff.
spiritual progress, 30, 31-32, 39, 40, 48, 137
stages in the spiritual life, three, 83ff.
struggle, 79, 80, 137

temperance, 84, 86
temptations, 22, 85-86
Thotokos, 75, 77, 95-96, 110, 120, 129, 138
Thermi of Lesvos, 102ff., 131ff.
Thessaloniki, 121, 142
 Othodox Missionary Society at, xi, 113, 124, 142

thoughts, 36, 47, 60, 79, 82-83, 85
Tradition, Holy, 120

Uganda, 108, 114-115, 124, 135
unbelief, 117

Vespers, 34, 116
vices, 78, 88
vigils, 27, 33, 82, 86
virginity, 85
virtues, xvii, 27, 51, 58, 83-84, 88, 121-122
vision of God, 83

Way of a Pilgrim, The, 49, 75, 76
watchfulness, 40, 82
wisdom, 60, 66, 82, 84, 137, 138

Zaire, 108, 114, 124, 143
zeal, 76, 81-82

THE OTHER VOLUMES OF CONSTANTINE CAVARNOS' SERIES *MODERN ORTHODOX SAINTS*

Vol. 1, ST. COSMAS AITOLOS

An account of the life, character, and message of St. Cosmas Aitolos (1714-1779) — great missionary, illuminator, and holy martyr of Greece. His teaching on God, Heaven and Hell, and his Prophecies, together with selections from his *Teachings (Didachai)*. 1971. 3rd edition, revised and considerably enlarged, 1985. Reprinted 1994. 118 pp. 6 illus.
ISBN 0-914744-65-8 (paperbound)

Vol. 2, ST. MACARIOS OF CORINTH

An account of the life, character, and message of St. Macarios (1731-1805) — Archbishop of Corinth, guardian of sacred Tradition, reviver of Orthodox mysticism (*hesychasm*), compiler of the *Philokalia*, spiritual striver, enlightener and guide, and trainer of martyrs — together with selections from three of his publications. 1972. Reprinted 1977. 2nd edition, 1993. 120 pp. 2 illus.   ISBN 0-914744-35-6 (paperbound)

Vol. 3, ST. NICODEMOS THE HAGIORITE

An account of the life, character, and teaching of St. Nicodemos the Hagiorite (1749-1809) — great theologian and teacher of the Orthodox Church, enlightener, reviver of hesychasm, moralist, canonist, hagiologist, and writer of liturgical poetry — together with a comprehensive list of his publications and selections from them. 1974. 2nd edition, 1969. Reprinted 1994. 168 pp., 3 illus.
ISBN 0-914744-17-8 (cloth); 0-914744-18-6 (paperbound)

Vol. 4, ST. NIKEPHOROS OF CHIOS

An account of the life, character, and message of St. Nikephoros of Chios (1750-1821) — outstanding writer of liturgical poetry and lives of saints, educator, spiritual striver, and trainer of martyrs — together with a comprehensive list of his publications, selections from them, and brief biographies of eleven neo-martyrs and other Orthodox saints who are treated in his works. 1976. 2nd, augmented edition, 1986. 124 pp., 2 illus.
ISBN 0-914744-74-7 (paperbound)

Vol. 5, ST. SERAPHIM OF SAROV

An account of the life, character, and message of St. Seraphim of Sarov (1759-1833_ — widely beloved mystic, healer, comforter, and spiritual guide — together with a very edifying Conversation with his disciple Nicholas Motovilov on the acquisition of the grace of the Holy Spirit and the Saint's Spiritual Counsels. This volume was written by Cavarnos in collaboration with Mary-Barbara Zeldin, a scholar with a wide acquaintance with Russian history and culture, proficient in the Russian language, and for many years Professor of Philosophy and Religion at Hollins College, Virginia. 1980. 2nd printing 1984. 3rd printing, 1993, 167 pp., 1 plate. ISBN 0-914744-48-8 (paperbound)

Vol. 6, ST. ARSENIOS OF PAROS

An account of the life, character, message, and miracles of St. Arsenios of Paros (1800-1877) — remarkable confessor, spiritual guide, teacher, ascetic, miracle-worker and healer — together with some of his counsels. 1978. 2nd, augmented edition, 1988. 124 pp., 4 illus.

ISBN 0-914744-80-1 (paperbound)

Vol. 7, ST. NECTARIOS OF AEGINA

An account of the life, character, and teaching of St. Nectarios (1846-1920) — educator, theologian, spiritual guide, miracle-worker and healer — together with a comprehensive list of his writings, selections from them and an essay on his teaching on God. 1981. 2nd, augmented edition, 1988. Reprinted 1995, 2000. 222 pp., 5 illus.

ISBN 0-914744-78-X (paperbound)

Vol. 8, ST. SAVVAS THE NEW (OF KALYMNOS)

An account of the life, character, message, and icons of St. Savvas the New Kalymnos (1862-1948) — remarkable ascetic, confessor, spiritual guide, miracle-worker and healer — together with his nine definitions of irreproachable monastic conduct. 1985. 144 pp., 23 full-page illus. Reprinted 1996. ISBN 0-914744-62-3 (paperbound)

Vol. 9, ST. METHODIA OF KIMOLOS

This volume is devoted to the most remarkable Greek woman saint of recent times, St. Methodia (1865-1908), patron saint of Kimolos, one of

the Cyclades Islands. It contains an account of the life of this remarkable ascetic, teacher of virtue, counselor, comforter, and spiritual healer, together with selected hymns, from the akolouthia in honor of her, selected sayings, and a description of Kimolos by Photios Kontoglou. 1987. 123 pp., 20 illus.
    ISBN 0-914744-75-5 (cloth); 0-914744-76-3 (paperbound)

Vol. 10, STS. RAPHAEL, NICHOLAS, AND IRENE OF LESVOS

Newly manifested Saints, who suffered Martyrdom by the Ottoman Turks in 1463 at the Monastery of the nativity of the Theotokos near the village of Thermi on the island of Lesvos. An account of their life, character, message, and miracles. 1990. 2nd printing 1994, 3rd printing 2000. 200 pp., 26 illus.
    ISBN 0-914744-87-9 (cloth); 0-914744-88-7 (paperbound)

Vol. 11, BLESSED ELDER PHILOTHEOS ZERVAKOS

Remarkable recent Confessor and Spiritual Guide, illuminating writer, and for half a century Abbot of the Monastery of Longovarda on the island of Paros. An account of his life, character, and thought. 1993. 240 pp. 10 illus.
    ISBN 0-914744-93-3 (cloth); 0-914744-94-1 (paperbound)

Vol. 12, BLESSED HERMIT PHILATEROS OF THE HOLY MOUNTAIN

Remarkable Ascetic and Mystic, faithful adherent of the ideals of the Kolyyvades Saints Macarios of Corinth and Nicodemos the Hagiorite. *Ca.* 1881-1961. An account of his life, character, and message. 1997. 125 pp., 13 illus.
    ISBN 1-884729-20-7 (cloth); 1-884729-21-5 (paperbound)

Vol. 13, BLESSED ELDER GABRIEL DIONYSIATIS (1886-1983)

Remarkable Confessor and Spiritual Guide, Profound Analyst of twentieth century society, inspiring Writer on many vital topics, and for forty years Abbot of the Monastery of Dionysiou at the Holy Mountain

of Athos. A comprehensive account of his life, character, thought, and works. 1999. 238 pp., 15 illus.
ISBN 1-884729-47-9 (cloth); 1-884729-48-7 (paperbound)